SYDNEY CONDRAY

O Gracious One

Psalm-Inspired
Prayers

TWENTY-THIRD PUBLICATIONS

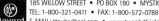

185 WILLOW STREET • PO BOX 180 • MYSTIC, CT 06355
TEL: 1-800-321-0411 • FAX: 1-800-572-0788
Bayard   E-MAIL: ttpubs@aol.com • www.twentythirdpublications.com

Twenty-Third Publications
A Division of Bayard
185 Willow Street
P.O. Box 180
Mystic, CT 06355
(860) 536-2611 or (800) 321-0411
www.twentythirdpublications.com
ISBN:1-58595-257-5

Library of Congress Catalog Card Number: 2002111928
Printed in the U.S.A.

Introduction

The Book of Psalms is a source of adoration, praise, courage and hope for many. These 150 prayer poems were inspired by these psalms. They are meant to give voice to our human condition and celebrate the mystery of God using inclusive language and contemporary imagery. They also include Jesus, the Christ, in the story of God's action in human history.

These poems may be prayed by an individual or used by a group. Where suitable, the poems are written in the plural, with the pronouns, "we," "us," and "our" instead of the singular "I," "me," and "mine," to encourage a conscious sense of connection with others. In addition, the word *kindom* has been substituted for *kingdom*. Kin-dom, as in kith and kin, implies family relationships and an ethic of mutual care. Kingdom, as in royal domain, conveys the idea of ruler and ruled with an ethic of duty or obligation.

There is no one right way to use these prayer poems. Allow the Spirit of the gracious Mystery to suggest their use in any particular situation. I hope these poems will be a source of enrichment, encouragement, and solace to all who use them for either personal or communal prayer.

1

The people who follow
  the gracious One
  know great happiness.
Yahweh's followers do no evil.
Neither do they join with those
  who scoff at God's way.

Rather, Yahweh's people are faithful.
They listen to this gracious Mystery
  with all their hearts.
They meditate on the Holy One
  both day and night.

Yahweh's followers are like trees
  planted by streams of living water.
Their leaves never wither
  and they bear good fruit in due season.

Whatever the circumstances,
  they know peace of heart
  for they dwell in the Holy One's love.
They rest secure in God's presence.

But those who do evil are not so.
They are like straw,
  blown this way and that by the wind.
They experience no rest.
They know no comfort
  in their inmost heart.

Like hungry wolves, they hunt
  but cannot fill themselves.
Like restless ghosts, they haunt
  but never touch true goodness.

They are condemned
   by their own actions
   and by their own preference
   exist outside
   the generous goodness
   of the Holy One.

Yet the gracious Mystery
   watches over all things
   and protects those
   who follow God's way.
But the way of evildoers
   will perish.

2

Gracious God, why do people persist
   in following selfish desires
   when such desires hurt others?
Why do governments insist
   on pursuing national agendas
   that bring harm to their neighbors?

The rulers of the earth act like gods.
The great of this planet conspire together.
They throw away all restraint
   saying: Let us ignore justice.
Let us break the laws that hamper us
   and keep us from our goals.

But the One-Who-Is laughs
   at their iniquitous attempts
   and cries bitter tears
   over their stupidity.

Then God warns them saying:
You will suffer the consequences
   of your actions.
I have declared my will.
My word is not broken
   with impunity.
Yahweh has declared
   to every human soul:
You are my beloved,
   my precious little ones,
   and I am Who-I-Am.
I create you and sustain you,
   and hold each of you in my heart.

Ask me for what you need.
Work for what is good.
I solemnly assure you
   the plans of evildoers
   will eventually come to nothing
   while you will know my goodness
   and be blessed.

But you rulers and powerful ones,
   listen to my word.
Reverence and follow my commands
   lest you suffer total destruction.

Happy are those who turn to me
   and follow my way of loving service.

3

O Holy One, we are so frightened
   and we feel so vulnerable.

We see many troubles coming to us.
Our fear says you do not care.
Our anxiety says you will not help us.
But we cry out:
Holy One, you are our stronghold.
You are our safety and our refuge.
Be our source of strength and courage!

Great God, we cried aloud to you
    and you answered us.
Thus we will lie down to sleep
    assured that our rest is secure
    for you keep us safe.
We will no longer fear
    the troubles that surround us

O God, rise up and liberate us.
Your presence banishes our fears.
Deliverance is yours, gracious One.
Rescue us and bring us home in joy.

4

Help us, O God, you who care for us.
In the past you heard our cry of need.
So, from your goodness, hear us now!

There are some who despise us
    and seek to discredit us.
They cause us great affliction.
These people crave worthless things
    and embrace lies.

But you, gracious One,
    choose each person.

You desire all of us to be your own.
Therefore, when our hearts are anxious
    we will dwell deeply on your favors.
We will count all the blessings
    you have given to us.

O people, know that Yahweh loves you.
Do not embrace false values.
Do not chase after worthless things.
Offer to God your poverty,
    your confusion, and your anxious heart.
You can utterly trust the Holy One.

There are many who pray for blessings
    and say to God: Look on us with kindness.
But you, gracious One, are more
    than many blessings for us.
You are our joy and our deepest gladness.

You are infinitely better
    than all the pleasures of soft living.
You are more satisfying
    than great wealth or power or prestige.
You alone, gracious One, are our peace.
Whether sleeping or waking,
    working or relaxing,
    you hold us secure in your loving care.

5

Great and loving One, heed our prayer.
Hear our cry and listen to our hearts
    for you are our God.
In the morning, we come with our need.
In the evening, we come with our poverty.

Throughout the day we wait upon you.
We wait with gratitude
   from sunrise to sunset
   while through the night we are filled
   with thanksgiving.

You do not delight in wickedness.
You tolerate no evil in your presence.
You take no pleasure in boasting.
You despise lies and deceit.
You abhor violence in all its forms.

Yahweh, we trust your steadfast love.
We look to your boundless mercy
   and worship you with all our hearts.
We bow before you in adoration.
We rejoice in You-Who-Are.
We give thanks
   that you are always with us.

Lead us, most gracious One,
   in your ways of truth and life.
Make a straight path before us
   because we are beset by problems.
Our frailties are daily stumbling blocks.
Our follies cause us constant misfortunes.
Save us from our failures.
Rescue us from our foolishness
   and keep us from stubbornness of heart.

O God, bring us all to rejoice in you.
Let us sing for joy
   from the refuge
   of your everlasting embrace.
Spread your steadfast mercy
   over all of us
   and train each of us
   in your loving kindness.

Then we shall each exalt and bless you.
We will praise you with all our hearts
   because you bless the poor
   and do not reject a contrite heart.

Great God, again show your goodness
   and hear this cry from our hearts.

6

Holy One, when we are anxious
   we wonder if you really exist.
When we are in great distress
   and you do not respond to our call,
   we sometimes think
   you are coldly distant
   or that you do not care.

Once more we are stricken
   and we call to you, Holy One.
Great God, answer our need!
Be kind to us
   for we are withering away.
Come and heal our fears.
We are besieged by mortal dread.
How long, O God, how long?

Rescue us! Yahweh, save our lives!
Save our lives
   out of your boundless mercy.
Save our lives
   because of your steadfast love.
In death we see no hope.
In death who can praise you?
And we are weary of pain.

We are beaten down with our struggles.
Even in the night
  we are crushed with anguish.
Tears of grief overflow.

But what is this?
Somehow we our consoled.
Our hearts are strengthened.
Our hope is revived.
You lifted us from dread.
You answered our prayer.

Fear retreats
  and doubt is put to flight.
Holy One, again
  we will sing your praise
  and give you thanks
  for your great kindness.

7

Merciful One, you are our refuge.
You are our place of calm and comfort.
We are laden by so many sorrows.
We are harried by so many worries.
They make our days wretched
  and our nights miserable.

Yahweh, hear our cry
  and rescue us from our troubles.
Otherwise, we are yesterday's news.
If you do not help,
  we will be destroyed.
Come, O God, save us!
Come, Holy One, rescue us!

You uphold the people
   who cling to you.
You save those
   who live your way of peace.
Let those who love you
   live in your presence.
Let those who follow your ways
   be gathered around you in joy.

You judge the peoples rightly.
Your judgment illumines the truth.
You know our inmost desires.
You know the thoughts of our minds
   and the motives of our hearts.
You judge both will and action.
You judge impartially.

The end is only sorrow
   for anyone who does evil.
There is only destruction
   for those who follow crooked paths.
The haughty and the selfish,
   slanderers, and thieves,
   all who are gorged with greed,
   who smolder with anger
   or are bitter with envy,
   bring disaster upon themselves.

O that evil might forever end
   and wickedness flourish no more.
O that all of us might turn to you
   and be transformed.

Then, great and gracious God,
   we shall all give you thanks
   for your infinite mercy and constant love.
Then we shall all sing praise
   to your glory forever.

8

Holy God, how wonderful you are,
   how striking and how beautiful.
We catch but a glimpse of you
   in the glory of your creation.

Your greatness is reflected
   by the heavens
   and your beauty is embodied
   by the earth.
Even infants and toddlers praise you.

You are Who-You-Are.
You are beyond all our concepts.
Nothing created can compare with you.
All beings fade into nothingness
   before you.

When we look at the sky
   which you created,
   and see the moon and stars
   which you made,
   we marvel in awe
   for we wonder: Who are we?
We are amazed
   that you are mindful of us.

Here we are, mere mortals,
   and you care for us.
You make us in your image
   and fashion us in your likeness.
You bestow honor upon us
   and share your glory with us.

You give us stewardship
   over the works of your hands.

You charge us to care
   for your creation:
   the land and sea,
   the plants and animals,
   the insects and fish,
   all things you have made.
You ask us to be mindful
   of your creation
   as you are mindful of each thing,
   for the benefit of all.

Gracious Yahweh, you who are our God,
Your glory interpenetrates all the earth.

9

We rejoice in you, gracious God.
We rejoice with every part our being
   and proclaim the wonderful things you do.
We will gladly sing of your goodness.
We will praise you with exultant hearts
   for you turned our struggles into joy.
You filled our empty hearts with delight.

A downcast spirit you have chased away
   as you poured out your blessings anew.
You judge rightly
   and your judgment is mercy.
The past is forgotten
   and sinful mistakes are erased.
Great One, you hold the whole universe
   in your loving care.
You are a sure refuge for the exploited.
You are a source of strength
   in troubled times.

Those who know you trust in you.
You are especially attentive
    to anyone who seeks you.
Gracious God, all peoples
    sing praise to you.

O nations, declare the Holy One's goodness.
O peoples, let all hear of God's greatness
    because Yahweh remembers the afflicted
    and answers the cry of the oppressed.

Adversity will be the lot
    of all who wrong others.
The people who do evil
    are finally caught
    in their own treachery.
Death is the destiny of any
    who choose wickedness.
Final ruin is the lot of those
    who reject the ways of Yahweh.

Though the world is sunk in misery
    and depravity stalks the land,
    the needy will not always be forgotten
    nor will the poor be crushed forever.

Rise up, gracious One,
    do not let wickedness prevail.
Come, Holy One!
Help each one
    to accept that we are mortal.

Great God, you are the One
    who lifts us from death.
You are the One who gives new life.
Touch and turn us all to you
    so we may find new life
    and our salvation.

10

Gracious and compassionate Yahweh,
    why are you so far away?
Why do you hide
    your presence from us?

This world is in such a mess.
The rich crush the poor.
The proud oppress the humble.
O God, turn every wicked scheme to dust.
Let all evil plans fail.

The people with power
    boast of their corrupt designs.
Those with money
    greedily do anything for more.

Holy One, these people
    totally renounce your ways.
In their pride they tell each other:
God favors us.
In their minds they think:
There is no God,
    and they continue to prosper.

Yahweh, these are the ones who scoff
    at the people who follow you.
They expect no adversity
    to come to themselves.
Their speech is full of lies and curses.
Malicious iniquity follows their steps.
They lay snares for the innocent
    and stealthily watch for their chance
    to entangle the helpless.
They lurk in dark places
    and watch to seize every advantage.

They entrap the poor
and murder them through their actions.
They think nothing will stop them

Rise up, great God, and lift your hand!
Do not leave the oppressed in their misery.
You are aware of their trouble and grief.
You know their anguish and feel their pain.
You are the helper of the helpless.
These little ones commit themselves to you.
Take them into your hand and defend them.

Turn the ruthless plans of the strong
to naught.
Seek out and destroy every iniquity.
You are the Holy One forever and ever.

11

The great and gracious God is our refuge.
Foolish people say: Run, hide from trouble.
Fly like the bird from adversity,
for threats are everywhere
and disaster can strike at anytime.

No one can escape from all afflictions.
Countless plans will go awry
and numberless projects fall apart.
Myriad hopes will melt away
while multitudes of dreams turn to dust.

But you, O God, are with us
in every moment.
You keep all of us in your care.

You know every circumstance
   of our lives.
You are aware of good and evil deeds.
You support the good
   and detest anything
   that harms your creation.

The effects of evil actions
   come home to roost for all of us.
But those who are far from you
   have no shelter,
   no security,
   and no hope
   when their lives are stricken
   by adversity.

But those who live your love
   are held in peace.
They are secure in your hand.
These will see your face.

12

Help us, gracious One,
   because evil multiplies.
No goodness seems to remain
   among the powerful.
Faith has disappeared
   and faithfulness has vanished.

All of our leaders lie.
They deceive and flatter each other.
They speak their treacherous designs
   from false hearts.
Honesty cannot be found.

Help us, merciful One,
   and silence the lies.
Destroy the deceptions.
Close the boastful mouths
   that say to each other:
We will get whatever we want
   and no one can stop us.

But now, I come! says our God.
I come to rescue and to save.
I will rescue the poor who are despoiled
   and save the needy who are trampled;
I will be their safe haven
   and give them the security
   they desperately desire.

Your promises, great God, are true.
Your words are absolutely reliable.
They are more precious than silver
   that is seven times refined.

You, gracious One,
   will protect your people.
You will preserve your little ones.
You will keep us from evil
   even while the wicked continue to prowl
   and praise vileness.

13

My God, how long will you forget us?
Will you cease to remember us forever?
How long will you hide yourself from us?
How long will pain fill our hearts,
   day and night, night and day?
How long will it be?

Everything keeps going wrong.
Listen to our cry and answer us.
Lighten our burdens.
Restore our courage.
Help us to live!

Holy One, do not let anxiety crush us
   nor emptiness prevail
   nor depression overwhelm,
   for we trust in you
   and your steadfast love.

Let us again be glad in your goodness
   and sing your kindness, most gracious One,
We will proclaim your bountiful generosity
   and rescuing power, for you are our God forever.

14

Foolish people say in their hearts:
There is no God,
   while they pursue corrupt desires.
They do terrible things without qualm.
These feel no disquiet
   when no one does what is right.

Yet, gracious One,
   you stay in our midst.
You seek the humble
   and search for the wise.
You look for your little ones
   who pursue your paths.
You look for anyone
   who follows your way.

But all have gone astray.
We are all alike in failing you.
No one is completely faithful.

The Holy One says:
"Don't you know? Are you ignorant?"
    to those who chase after evil.
God says: "You will know great terror"
    to those who live by robbing
    and exploiting others.
Indeed, these will know great terror.

But you, Yahweh, are with those
    who follow your way.
Evildoers may injure the humble
    but the Holy One is with them.
The merciful One is their refuge,
    their salvation,
    and will be their final vindication.

Gracious One, we earnestly seek you.
We ask you to touch and heal our world.
We ask you to turn foolish people to you
    so they may be transformed.

We will be so glad when justice is restored,
    when every heart is touched by your love
    and peace prevails.

Blessed be our great and gracious God,
    the creator of the universe,
    who accomplishes all these things.

15

Great God, who may live
  in your presence?
Who may stand with honor
  before your face?
The people who follow your way
  and do what is right.
They who speak the truth
  and are honest in daily affairs.

The people who do not slander
  and do not wrong their neighbor.
They who despise wickedness
  and rejoice in goodness.
Those who honor the ones
  who reverence you, most gracious One.

The people who keep their promises
  and are faithful to their word
  no matter what the cost to themselves.
Those who do not take bribes
  to favor some over others.
They who lend generously
  without expecting a return.
The people who are merciful
  as you are merciful.

The ones who do these things
  live always in your presence
  and dwell secure
  in your everlasting arms.

16

Great God, you show us the path to life
   and will guide us into joy forever.
Protect us, gracious One,
   for we take refuge in you.
We trust you and say to you:
You are our God.

All good comes from you.
We admire the people
   who follow your ways.
To be with them is our delight.

As for those who make a god
   of pleasure or money,
   of power or prestige,
   or any other thing,
   they bring many troubles
   on themselves as well as on others.
They multiply their sorrows.
We will not follow their example.
We will not make 'things' our god.

You, Yahweh, are our chosen God.
You are all we have
   and you provide all that we need.
Our future is only in you.
How wonderful are your gifts.
How good you are.

I thank you, Holy One,
   who leads us in right paths.
I thank you who, even at night,
   gives good counsel
    in the depth of our hearts.

I praise you
   who are unceasingly with us.
I rejoice in you
   who are always near.
Nothing will shake us.

Therefore our hearts are glad
   and our spirits rejoice.
You protect us from the power of death.
You will not let us be overwhelmed
   by any kind of evil.
Indeed, you show us
   that your essence is fullness.
It is fullness of life.
Your presence is joy, running over.

Within your loving embrace
   we are completely satisfied.
We know the glory of Who-You-Are.
We know you as you are.
Blessed be God forever. Amen.

17

Hear us, great God.
   and listen to our cry!
Be attentive to our plea.
You know our hearts.
You know how much
   we want to please you.
We seek your will
   and do our best to walk your paths.

Holy One, we cry to you
   because you do answer us.

Gracious One, hear us
   and reveal your steadfast care.
Hold us close and we are secure.
Nothing can touch us.
Nothing will hurt us.
Guard us as the apple of your eye.
Keep us safe in your loving embrace
   for you are our God.

Yet we feel besieged
   by treacherous feelings.
Hurtful thoughts pursue us night and day.
We are surrounded by doubt and fear.
There is no relief.
There is no surcease.
They are like lions waiting to strike,
   trying to destroy us.

Come, Holy One!
Confront and defeat them.
Save us from their power over us.
Rescue us from their influence on us.
Totally erase them.
Then we shall rejoice once more
   in your presence.
Beholding you will again
   fill us with joy.

18

Great God, you are our savior.
You are our rock and our fortress.
Gracious God, you are our deliverer.
You are our protection from evil.
With you, we are safe.

We call upon you and you answer us.
We reach out to you and you are there.
You give us support in all our troubles.
We praise you, Yahweh,
    for your great goodness to us.

We feared death and you delivered us.
We faced extermination and you saved us.
In our fear and despair, we called to you
    and you heard our cry.

The hurts and failures,
    the sorrows and frustrations,
    the tragedies and calamities of life,
    will not destroy us.
You are always near.
You will reach out and save us.

Through earthquakes and floods,
    thick darkness and lightning flashes,
    perilous winds and blinding rains,
    you lead us and keep us safe.
We remain secure in your steadfast love.

Your word is our ever-present guide.
You shield us from disaster
    and protect us from destructive choices
    because we keep your ways.

You show yourself as faithful
    to those who are faithful.
You show yourself as good
    to those who are good.
You show yourself as truth
    to those who are honest.
But you turn away
    from those who are perverse.

You save the humble
 and humble the proud.

Yahweh, how great you are!
How wonderful your deeds.
How dependable your words.
You are a safe haven
 for all who take refuge in you.
You alone are God.
You alone keep us safe
You alone support us in our need.

We are the delight of your heart
 for you are our God.
The gracious Mystery lives!
And we praise you.

Glorious One, you give us light
 to see the true
 and freedom to choose the good.
You surround us with strength
 and inspire us with love.
You trust us with your purposes
 and provide your enduring help.
You commission us to accomplish
 your desires for this earth.
You put gifts in our hands
 to share with others.

Great God, we love you.
We proclaim your greatness
 because you rescue us.
You deliver us from death
 and help us in every struggle.

So we rejoice in you
 among the people
 and sing of your faithful care
 to all who will listen.

Thus we celebrate
   your presence in our lives,
   while the whole world
   proclaims your goodness.

19

The heavens proclaim your glory, O God.
The universe reveals your infinite splendor.
How plainly it declares your creativity.
How marvelously it shows your power.

As day follows day,
your creatures pour out their praise.
As night follows night,
your creation joyfully extols you.
Though no speech is used
or sound is heard,
their message goes out
to the whole world
   and their meaning is revealed
   to the ends of the earth.

You hold the sun on its path
   and moon on its course.
You keep the planets in their orbits.
Like a radiant bride
   the sun rises in the morning
   and like a joyful athlete
   it races across the sky.
Nothing is hidden in its light.
Each day you make a path for us.
Your words give strength.
Your ways are trustworthy.
Your paths are clear.

Your presence revives our spirits.
Your loving kindness brings joy to us.

Your truth is such wisdom
    that even toddlers understand.
Reverence for you is right
    and will endure forever.

Your justice is mercy on all flesh.
Though sometimes deeper
    than our thoughts can follow,
    all your judgments are good.
They will be vindicated
    in your eternal light.

You are more desirable than any riches.
You are sweeter than honey from the comb.
You are more delicious than well-aged wine
    and more satisfying than the finest food.

You give us knowledge of your desires
    and, by your love, teach us your ways.
Because of you, we know great gladness.
In you our joy is complete.

But, most gracious One,
    we will never really know all our faults.
Deliver us from stupid misunderstandings
    and keep us from foolish mistakes.
Save us from deliberate sins.
Preserve us from pride and deceit.
Do not let evil overwhelm us.
Wrap us in your merciful kindness.

Then nothing will separate us from you
    nor break our bonds of our friendship
    with each other.

Let these thoughts be acceptable to you.
May our words and actions
    find favor in your sight.
You are our only security and our savior.
May you be reverenced, rejoiced in,
    and loved forever.

20

May you, Yahweh,
    answer us in times of trouble.
May you support and protect us.
May you send us help in time of need.
Always be with us with your wisdom
    and grant us your strength.

May you remember our dedication to you.
Our hearts' desire is to please you.
Our only purpose is to serve you.
May we know your acceptance
    and rest in you love.

O God, hear our plea!
Then we will shout with joy
    and dance our thanksgiving,
    for you have answered our prayer.
We shall not be overcome.
Some trust in money
    to provide their security.
Some trust in military power
    to protect them.
Others use force to gain their desires.
While more rely on technology
to provide for all their needs.

But such things always fail
    to satisfy our deepest desires.
They prove they are not the solution
    to the real problems of our world.
They shall all collapse
    and fall to nothing in the end.

But even if we founder, we shall rise.
O God, we will rest secure
    in your gracious goodness.
Hear our prayer, most gracious One,
    and answer our cry to you.

21

Gracious God, we are grateful
    because you help each of us.
We rejoice because you provide
    so much more than we can truly imagine.

You give us our heart's desire.
You answer our requests.
You respect and renew us.
You bestow great blessings.
You give us purpose for our days
    and meaning for our lives.
You respond to our deepest needs.

We ask for security
    and you enfold us with love.
We ask for protection
    and you fill us with peace.

We ask fulfillment of our desires
    and you give us life
    abundantly,
    pressed down,
    shaken together,
    and running over.

We are glad with the joy
    of your presence among us.
We trust you.
When your abiding love supports us
    we shall not be moved.

You show us
    the things we need to change
    in ourselves and in our world.
You convict us of our failures
    and lay bare our sins.
Then in your mercy you forget them.

You cancel failure's offspring
    so they do not overwhelm us.
Sin's malevolence will not destroy us.
Mistakes will not deflect the good
    you will draw forth from our blunders.

We indeed praise you, O God,
    for your infinite love.
We sing of your wisdom
    and give thanks for your care.
We proclaim your mercy
    in the company of the just
    and in the assembly
    of all your people.

22

Great God, our God,
   why do you abandon us?
We desperately call out for your help.
Still, you do not answer.
Day and night we cry out to you.
But you do not respond.

You are Yahweh, our God.
You are the holy One-Who-Is.
You are the One whom the saints praise
   and the people worship.
You are the One our ancestors trusted.

Again and again, you answered their need.
They called out to you and you saved them.
They had faith in you and you rescued them.
You helped them prevail over
   all their troubles and woes.

But we have become like rubbish.
We are dried leaves tossed in the wind.
We are scorned by the righteous
   and ignored by the satisfied.
We are despised by those who spurn us.

They shake their heads and say:
You trusted God. Let God save you.
If you are Yahweh's delight,
   let Yahweh rescue you.
Gracious One, you knew us
   from before we were born.
You cared for us from our birth.
We were yours from infancy.
You have always been our God.

Holy One, be close to us
for trouble is very near.
There is no one to help but you.
We are surrounded by hatred.
We are hunted by violence.

Our strength is gone.
We are like water
flowing into desert sand.
We are poured out as a libation
onto the ground.

Our bones are jelly.
Our hearts are melted wax.
Our voice is dried up.
We are like the dead
who lie in the dust.

Evil surrounds us
like a pack of wild dogs.
They are savage predators
ready to attack.
Evil wants to tear us
limb from limb.

Hostile stares are directed at us.
Abusive remarks are flung at us.
These strip the last shreds
of human dignity from us.
People bet on our destruction.

Great God, do not forsake us!
Come quickly and rescue us.
Holy One, save us!
Save us from the powers of evil.
Preserve our lives and rescue us.
We are made helpless by this assault.
We are powerless in our distress.

Save us! And we will tell the people
    what you have done.
Rescue us! And we will praise you
    in the assembly of your people.

You who reverence Yahweh,
    praise our gracious God.
All you children of the Most High,
    give God thanks.

Worship our God with joy and gratitude,
    for Yahweh does not abandon us.
Rather, the gracious One hears our cry
    and releases us.

We will praise you
    in the gathered assembly
    for your great goodness.
We will keep our promises to you,
    in the company
    of those who worship you.

The poor will be filled to overflowing
    and they who seek you will find you.
They will live with you, forever.

O God, all the nations
    will remember you
    and will turn to you with joy.
Great God, every people
    of this world will worship you,
    for all creation belongs to you.
All creation, indeed, belongs to you.

Yahweh is creator and sustainer,
    reclaimer and sanctifier
    of the whole universe.

All the great of this world
    will adore you.
All the nations of this planet
    will glorify you.

All who sleep in the earth
    will reverence you.
All who are alive today
    will praise you.
Future generations
    will be told of you.
Peoples yet to be born
    will proclaim you as their savior.

23

The gracious Mystery is a faithful friend.
The Holy One is our steadfast guardian
The merciful One is our trustworthy guide.

Great God, you provide for every need.
You bring us serenity and joy.
You lead us to security of spirit.
Your gift is deep assurance
    and peace of soul.

You give us new strength
    as you sustain us in your way of truth.
You are our peace on the path of life.
You are always near.

We shall not fear
    even when we are plunged
    into deep darkness
    or drawn into dangerous places.

We will not be afraid
   when death itself is present,
   for you are with us to uphold us.

You are courage when we are fearful.
You are strength when we are burdened.
You are comfort when we are afflicted.
You are unexpected joy
   when we are empty and alone.

We know your goodness.
We know your kindness.
Your love shall be with us
   all the days of our lives.
And we shall dwell
   in your presence forever.

24

The universe, gracious One,
   is your creation.
This world is your handiwork.
All living creatures come from you.
You form all things
   and keep all things in being.
You are the foundation of our cosmos.
Nothing exists beyond your sustaining care.

Great God, who are they who serve you?
Who are they who truly love you?
The people who desire to live your purposes.
The ones whose hands do your work.
The ones whose hearts follow your way.
They who serve justice and promote peace.

The people who walk humbly with you
throughout their days.

You are their blessing, Holy One.
You are their vindication and their joy.
These are the people who belong to you.
These are the ones who will live with you forever.

Open your minds, O people!
Receive the One-Who-Is!
Who is this glorious Mystery?
Yahweh is the One-Who-Is,
the Holy One, who is wonder and light.

Open your hearts, O people!
Receive the One-Who-Is-With-Us!
Who is this gracious Mystery?
Yahweh is the One-Who-Is-With-Us,
the Holy One, who is wisdom and life.

Open your whole being, O people!
Receive the One-Who-Is-For-Us!
Who is this generous Mystery?
Yahweh is the One-Who-Is-For-Us,
the Holy One, who is mercy and joy forever.

25

To you, Yahweh, we open our hearts.
In you, O God, we trust.
Save us from our failures.
Rescue us from our doubts.
Release us from our fears.

Those who trust in you
    can rest secure.
They who place their faith in you
    will find true peace of heart.

Gracious God, we ask your mercy.
We need your assisstance.
Teach us your ways.
Make your paths known to us.
Support and protect us
    so we may live your truth,
        for you are the God who saves.

Holy One, we will always trust you.
Remember your mercy toward us.
Remember your fidelity and love.
For we have seen your merciful love
    that you gave to our ancestors
    again and again.
We have known your generous love
    many times in our own lives.

Great God, you are compassion itself.
You are truth itself.
Therefore, even though we are
    limited in our understandings
    and foolish in our actions,
    you will not cease to teach us
    what is right.
And because we are weak
    you will strengthen us.

You lead the humble in your truth.
You show them your will.
You bless the ones who keep your ways.
You bless them with your abiding love
    and faithful care.

From your infinite compassion,
  forgive our sins for they are many.
Teach us to reverence you
  and show us the paths we should follow.
Then we will abide in security of heart.
Abundant peace will fill us.
This is the legacy we shall leave
  to future generations.

Great and gracious One,
  your friendship is known
  by those who reverence you.
You are a steadfast companion
  in their inmost heart.
You affirm your promises to them
  and give them peace.

Yahweh, we look to you for help.
We look to you at all times
  and you rescue us from danger.
Turn again and be gracious to us,
  for we are alone and struggling.

Lift our anxiety and save us from fear.
Consider our sufferings.
See our troubles and forgive our failures.
You know the temptations that besiege us.
You see the problems that surround us.
Look at how much they afflict us.

Be our protection and restore us to yourself.
Watch over us and hold us close,
Great God, because we trust in you.
Save us from all tribulation.

26

Gracious God, you probe us
and you know us.
You know our bitter failures
and you know our discontents.
You know our terrible weaknesses.
You also see our greatest hopes
and most generous desires.

Holy One, look upon our finest hopes.
Consider our most worthy desires.
Do not remember our foolish mistakes.
We look to your enduring love.
You are our surest hope.
We trust you to lead us, faithfully.

Great God, keep us from chasing
after worthless things.
Turn us away from hypocrisy
and do not let us fall into sin of any kind.
We repent of every evil thought.
We deplore each foolish word
and reject all wicked actions.
We renounce everything
which does not please you.

Yahweh, wash away our sins
and free us of our faults.
Let our hands be purified of every failing.
Let our hearts be cleansed of all iniquity.
Free our bodies from wrongdoing.
Keep our thoughts from offending you.
Then we will sing for joy
and we will tell everyone
of your wondrous deeds.

Gracious One, we love you
  with all our hearts.
We love your world and your people
  in which you so deeply abide.
You are so totally caring,
  so generously loving,
  so fiercely compassionate,
  toward each of us and all of us.

Therefore, again we ask you
  to keep us from sin
  and rescue us from our own foolishness.
Spare us the fate of those
  who knowingly and willingly
  murder, lie, and steal,
  who are always ready to seek
  their own advantage.

But for us, help us walk
  in the integrity of your truth
  and be ever ready to love.
Help us to reach out
  to even the littlest and least,
  the most despised and repulsive,
  in the same way that you love us.
Yes, great God, help us to reach out
  to all, in the same way that you love us.

Rescue us, all of us, gracious One.
In you we stand on solid ground.
Thus with all your peoples,
  we will bless you forever.

27

Yahweh is our light and our salvation.
We shall not fear.
Yahweh protects us from every danger.
We shall not be afraid.
O God, no evil in this world
    can destroy those who dwell
    in your loving embrace.

Holy One, we trust in you.
When problems assail us, we will not fear.
When afflictions abound, we will not be dismayed
When woes beat us down,
    yes, even when our whole world
    is crumbling, we will not be afraid.
As we sink into the darkness of death,
    gracious One, we will still trust you.

We ask for only one thing.
Holy One, we want only this:
To live in your presence
    all the days of our lives.
May we celebrate your goodness
    and always know your guidance.

Great God, shelter us when troubles come.
Keep us safe in your presence.
Hold us secure in the palm of your hand.
Thus we will overcome our afflictions.
We will master our problems
    and surmount the woes that surround us.
We will offer thanks with shouts of joy.
We will sing in praise of our God.

Great God, continue to hear us
    when we cry out to you.

Be gracious and answer us.
When our hearts hear your call,
    we will seek you and come to you.
Do not hide yourself from us.

Yet we can still be worried.
We can still be uncertain and confused.
So, merciful God, our savior,
    do not turn away.
You who are our help, do not leave us.
Even if our families should abandon us,
    do not forsake us.

Great God, teach us your ways
    and lead us with tranquil hearts
    through all of our troubles.
Do not leave us in the midst of distress.
Do not let malice and violence prevail.

We know we shall live
    to see Yahweh's mercy.
Trust and wait for the One-Who-Is.
Be strong, have courage,
    and wait for our God.

We trust in you, most gracious One.
Yes, we will trust and wait for you.

28

Yahweh, most gracious One, hear us!
You, who are our refuge, listen to us!
For if you do not answer
    we will be pulled into a maelstrom.
We will be dead and quickly forgotten.

So, swiftly come to us
    when we cry to you,
    when we are in such desperate need,
    when we lift our hands in supplication,
    when we turn to your holy presence.

Do not let us fall into evil ways.
Save us from hypocrisy and malice.
Keep us from hatred and violence of heart.
Do not let us be like people
    who ignore you and forget you.
These have no future.
They cut themselves off
    from the source of life.
They are like the walking dead.
They receive what they have chosen.

Great God, we will bless you
    with immense joy
    because you heard our anguished plea.
You protected and strengthened us.

We trusted in you with our whole being.
So now we exult in your help
    with our whole heart.
Our spirits are filled with gratitude
    and we praise you with gladsome songs.

Gracious One, you protect your people.
You defend your chosen ones.
You renew your little ones.
Holy One, save all your people.
Bless all who belong to you
    with abundant life.
You are our faithful guardian
    and guide forever.

29

Sing praise to Yahweh,
  all you creatures of the earth.
Sing praise to our God,
  all you peoples of this world.
Praise our God of wonder and light.
Give praise to the One-Who-Is.
Adore the Holy One with heartfelt gratitude.

Holy One, the vastness of the oceans
  suggests your greatness.
Their intricate, teaming life-forms
  illumine your creativity.
Their stormy winds and crashing waves
  reflect your awesome power.

Oh God, you are aliveness itself.
You are aliveness
  in all its mystery and majesty.
Your aliveness blazes forth,
  like the summer sun.
You are the fructifying, sustaining source
  of existence for every creature.

Your aliveness brings forth like a mother.
You give birth to every creature
  in all their marvelous forms,
    from tiny lichens to great forests,
    from protozoa to elephants and whales.

Your aliveness moves
  with inexorable power,
    like colliding tectonic plates,
    raising up mountains to the sky
    and opening the depths
    in ocean trenches.

Your aliveness bursts forth like water,
    like water from a broken dam
    sweeping over and through everything
    in its roiling, roaring path.

Your aliveness flashes forth,
    like lightening across the sky,
    enlightening our consciousness
    and illuminating your presence with us.

Gracious One, you are beingness itself.
Like thunder shakes the earth,
    the intensity of your beingness
    shakes the very foundation of our souls.

You are beingness, more intense
    than the fiery heart of the hottest star.
And all creation cries out
    in wonder at your glory.

By your desire you create all things.
By your choice you sustain
    all things in being,
    from the outermost reaches
    to the innermost depths.
Nothing exists outside of you.

Great God, give strength to your people
    and bless them with your peace.

30

We proclaim your goodness, Holy One,
    because you are with us.
We rejoice in you because you rescue us.
We give you thanks because you renew us.

Great God, we cried out to you
  and you healed us.
You delivered us from the depths
  of our distress.
You restored us and saved us from destruction.

Sing praise to Yahweh,
  all you faithful ones.
Remember what the Holy One has done
  and exult in God's loving care.

Though Yahweh abhors our sins,
  still God's mercy is poured out
  on all generations.
We may fill the night with lament.
But joy comes in the morning.

We felt secure in our prosperity
  when our lives were going well.
We said to ourselves:
We shall not be troubled.
Yahweh will protect us
  and keep us safe.

But then, Holy One, things went wrong.
Disaster, disease, and death followed.
You hid yourself from us
  and we grew afraid.
Again we turned to you
  and called out to you.
We begged you for your help.

We asked: If we are dead,
  how can we serve you?
Can the dead speak
  of your unfailing goodness?
Can dust and ashes
  accomplish your purposes?

Who will proclaim your faithfulness?
Hear us, O gracious One, and help us!

Then suddenly you change our grief
    into radiant joy.
You turn our fear into new courage.
Our sorrow is transformed into dancing
    and you clothe us with new life.
So now we cannot be silent.
We must shout our grateful praise.

Great and gracious God, you are our God!
We will give thanks to you forever.

31

O God, once more we call out to you.
Again we seek refuge in you.
Save us from our distress.
And in your mercy, deliver us.
Hear our anguished cry.
Come and save us, quickly!

Be our security in the midst of woe.
Be our strong defense against all evil.
You are, indeed, our rock
    and our stronghold.

Because of your goodness, lead us.
Out of your compassion, guide us.
We are trapped by terrible anxiety.
We are entangled in a deadly snare of fear.

Holy One, you are our fortress
    and our protection.
Into your loving care
    we commend our spirits.
You will release us
    from this terrible turmoil.
You will rescue us
    from these lethal assaults.

O gracious and faithful God,
    have pity on all people who are
    trapped by crushing anxiety.
Have mercy on all those who are
    entangled in deadly fear.
May they turn to you with confident trust
    and may their faith in you be vindicated.

Holy One, help all of us to trust you.
See our afflictions and heed our anxieties.
Deliver us from our fears and give us peace.
Then we will rejoice in your steadfast love.

O Holy One, again we ask your mercy
    for we remain haunted by apprehension.
Our eyes are swollen from many tears.
We are worn out by distress.
We are exhausted by tensions.
Our stamina fails and strength melts away.

We feel like puppets
    with fear pulling the strings.
Others turn away in contempt.
Those we counted as friends
    run away from us.
Even strangers keep their distance.

We are ignored, denied, made into nothing.
We are forgotten, like those long dead.

We are broken vessels around which
    the wind whispers dread.
We are tiny bits of wood tossed about
    on floods of turmoil.
There is no one and nothing to cling to.

Great God, be with us and save us.
Do not let us fall away from you.
In your steadfast love, keep us safe.

May our anxieties dissolve to naught.
May all our fears be put to flight.
Silence the whispering dread.
Abolish the panic.

When we are beset by dread,
    help us to remember all the good things
    you have given to us.
When panic strikes and fear overwhelms,
    help us to rest in your faithful care.

Yahweh, we reach out to you
    and you will save us once more.
O how great is your goodness.
How marvelous is your kindness
    toward those who reverence you.

You shelter and protect
    anyone who turns to you.
You hold each in deep peace,
    beyond all comprehending.
Nothing can distress their inmost heart.

Worship our God, all you peoples,
    for Yahweh preserves
    those who are faithful.
Give thanks to our God, all you nations,
    for our gracious One protects the humble
    and saves the contrite of heart.

Be strong and wait with courage
    all you who hope in the One-Who-Is.
Be strong and wait, my soul.

32

Those whose sins are forgiven
    are at peace.
Those whose wrongs are pardoned
    rest secure.
Blessed are all who do not lie.
Happy are they who do not deceive.

When we try to hide our sins,
    we are always anxious.
When we seek to cover our failures,
    we are heavy laden.
Day and night we are pursued
    by dread of their discovery.
Night and day we are burdened
    by fear of their revelation.

Then, gracious One, we confessed our sins.
We acknowledged our failures.
We did not conceal our wrongdoings.
We said: Holy One, we have sinned.
We have failed you and hurt others.
We have even injured ourselves
    by our misdeeds.

We abhor our wrongful deeds
    and will change our actions.
And, amazingly, you pardoned everything.
Thus, gracious God, we are set free.

Therefore, turn to God,
    you who have sinned and fallen short.
Fear not, and turn to Yahweh.
Ask forgiveness and you will receive it.
Seek mercy and you will find it,
    for Yahweh is the gracious One-Who-Is.

Humbly implore Yahweh for a new heart.
Beseech the holy Mystery for a new spirit.
Then, when troubles come suddenly,
    as a tornado in the night,
    you will not be overwhelmed.

Yahweh will be your security.
The Holy One will be your safety
    amid the tempest.
Our God will be your steadfast shelter
    at the center of any storm.

Gracious One, we shout for joy
    because of your great goodness.
We sing with gladness and thanksgiving.
We sing because you are merciful.
We shout gladness because you protect us.
We rejoice because you pardon
    all our sins.

You say to us: I will teach you
    the way you should go.
I will support you and advise you.
I will be with you in every circumstance.

Do not be obstinate, like mules
    who fight guidance.
Do not act recklessly or willfully.
Many are the sorrows of the stubborn
    and many the regrets of the defiant.

Those who pursue evil ways
    will suffer the consequences of their choices.
But they who trust in you
    are preserved by your constant love.

You who reverence our God, be glad.
You who love our God, rejoice.
Because Yahweh's kindness
    surrounds you.

All of you who willingly follow
Yahweh's paths,
    exalt and give thanks,
    for you are enfolded
    in abundant life forever.

33

Rejoice in Yahweh, all you peoples.
Again I say, rejoice.
Gladness is fitting and praise is proper
    for all the gracious One has done.

Give thanks to our God with music.
Make melodies of joy
    with all stringed instruments,
    with guitar and violin,
    with piano and balalaika.

Sing a new song with the banjo and harp.
Give the Holy One praise
    with shouts of delight
    for Yahweh's word is true
    and all God's deeds are good.

Great God, you love virtue and justice
    and the earth is full of your steadfast love.
Through your wisdom all things come to be.
Without your constant care nothing exists.
By your will the universe was made
    and by the breath of your Spirit
    all the hosts of heaven and earth
    were formed.
All your words are creative
    and all your works are just.

You formed the galaxies
    and set their motion.
You shaped the planets
    in all their diversity.
You created this world
    from your heart's deepest desire.
All your words are helpful
    and all your works are of great value.

Let all the earth reverence our God.
Let the inhabitants of our globe honor you.
For you have created a wondrous world,
    a world of intricately interconnected life,
    a world full of beauty.

Great God, before you
    human knowledge is as nothing.
You work constantly to bring forth the good
    and frustrate the perverse plans
    of the nations.
The fullness of your wisdom is forever.
The thoughts of your heart are manifested
    to anyone who seeks you.

Happy are those whose God is Yahweh.
Happy the people who follow your way.
Yahweh knows all of humankind.

Each individual is enfolded
    in God's singular love.

Gracious One, you fathom
    the deepest part of each person.
You know everything each one thinks and feels.
You are aware of what each one says and does.
Nothing is unknown to you.
Power will not save us.
Strength cannot free us.
Technology will not rescue us.

Gracious God, you watch over the people,
    the people who reverence you.
You watch over your little ones
    who trust in your steadfast love.
You deliver them from death
    and preserve them in times of adversity.

Our hope is in Yahweh.
The Holy One is our help.
The gracious One is our protector.
We are glad in the One-Who-Is.
We trust in you who are our God.

Most holy and gracious One,
    let your faithful love be upon us.
We place our hope in you.

34

Gracious One, we will always adore you.
We will continuously rejoice in you.
We will praise you for all you have done.
Let anyone who is fearful
    hear and be glad.
Let those who are threatened
    be secure.

O give thanks to our God with us.
Let us exult in Yahweh together.
We looked for our God and God answered.
We were freed from our dread.

Look to the Holy One
    and be radiant with joy.
    for the people who trust in Yahweh
    will never be disappointed.

When we were helpless
    we called out to God
    and we were rescued
    from all our troubles.

Holy One, you surround with love
    those who follow your paths
    and you deliver them from their anguish.

O taste and see the goodness of God.
Happy are all who take refuge in Yahweh.
Reverence the Holy One, all you peoples.
Worship and rejoice in our God forever.

35

Great God, I am so angry
 and at my wit's end.
I feel totally frustrated.
I am in such a sorry state.
I don't know where to turn.
I can only turn to you, my God.

Everything is collapsing around me.
Everything is going wrong
 and falling apart.
I don't know what to do.
Come! Help me!

Gracious One, all my plans, my hopes
 and dreams are turned to ashes.
Why is this happening?
Why?
At every turn I am besieged
 and confounded.

Great God, don't let my life
 be wasted like this.
Let these troubles blow away
 like dust in the wind.
Drive them away
 with your creative power.
Chase this melancholy from my soul
 for it entangles my spirit.
I have fallen into a pit
 and there is no way out.

O free me from this snare.
Pull me from this trap.
Then my spirit shall
 again rejoice in you.

My mind shall exult
  in your deliverance.
My body, too, will celebrate in joy.

With all my heart I will say to you:
Great God, there is no one like you.
You deliver the weak from their distress.
You support the needy
  and keep them at peace
  even in the midst of pain.

Yet I am still harassed
I am still ridiculed and insulted.
I want to hit back.
I want to harm those who harm me.
I want the people who harm me
  to be punished.

These are people who tell lies about me.
They return evil for the good I do them.
These are people who laugh
  at my stumbling.
They mock me and make fun of me.
They glare at me with hate.
I want them to pay for their offenses.

Gracious One, how long
  must I endure this violence?
Rescue me from these attacks.
Do not let these people
  devour me with their lies.
Do not let them gloat over me.
  or mock me in my pain.

Save my life from these lions
  and I will publicly thank you.
I will praise you before them all,
  in the great assembly of your people.

You see my affliction
   and know all things.
Do not be silent!
Be not far from me!
Hurry and help me
   for you are my only refuge.
You are my strength and my hope.
Rescue me from this swamp.
Do not let me be swallowed up
   by this quicksand.

Bless the people who support me.
Vindicate their trust in me.
Let them exult and say with joy:
How great is our God
   who rescues the needy
   and delivers them from all their woes.

I, too, will proclaim your goodness.
I will praise you all the day long.

36

Merciful God, so many people
   are caught up in selfishness.
They are blinded by their wrongdoing
   and so, are headed for ruin.

These have no thought for anything
   beyond themselves.
They have no awareness of you
   nor concern for the well being of others.
They deceive themselves
   and tell themselves what they do is good.

These, too, assure themselves
   that their lies will not be uncovered.
They are sure their manipulations
   will not come to light.
So they continue to plot evil,
   even on their beds at night.
They are set on paths that bring harm to all.
Odious thoughts are not rejected
   and corrupt deeds
   are their constant companions.

But, great God, your steadfast love
   extends to every nook of our world
   and to every cranny of your creation.
Your faithful care abounds
   in ways we do not fathom.
You lovingly work at depths
   beyond our profoundest thoughts.

Gracious One, your goodness is greater
   than the whole expanse of our universe.
Your mercy is deeper
   than the deepest deep of space.
You create and sustain all living things.
You encompass everything
   with your saving power.

O God, how precious is your faithful love.
Every person can find refuge
   in the warmth of your tender embrace.
Your abiding presence is a rich feast
   satisfying our deepest hungers.
Your goodness is a river of delight
   satisfying our greatest thirsts.
Your mercy is a fountain of life
   for all who turn to you.
It is in your light that we see light.

Merciful One, continue to pour
    your steadfast love on your creation.
Generous One, let your goodness
    flow out to all in need.
Strengthen those who love you
    and sustain those who do your will.
Defend your little ones.
Keep them from harm
    and deliver them from evil.

Let those who are trapped in selfishness
    find their way to you.
And may those who lie prostrate in sin
    be transformed by the creative power
    of your love.

Then all will exclaim: Hosanna!
    in the great circle of your mercy
    and proclaim your goodness
    in everlasting delight.

37

Do not fret about people who do wrong.
Do not be jealous of their lives
    for they will not long endure.
Like the grass which withers
    in winter frosts, they too will die.
Like every created thing, they will pass away.

Rather, trust in Yahweh and do good.
Live peacefully and honestly.
Seek your happiness
    only in the gracious Mystery
    and you will receive
    your most heartfelt desire.

Be still and wait for Yahweh.
Wait patiently for the One-Who-Is.
Trust in Yahweh and Yahweh will help you.
Commit yourself to God and God will act.
You will find joy and peace of heart.
Even in the midst of distress,
    you will be serene.
Your very being will shine gloriously,
    like the noonday sun.

Be patient and trust in Yahweh.
Let go of your worry and refrain from anger.
Both only bring more and greater problems.
Do not be anxious over those who prosper
    through dishonest means.
Do not be troubled by those who pursue
    wicked schemes.

Those who trust in Yahweh
    will inherit eternal life
    while those who persist in evil ways
    will simply turn to dust.
They will disappear and not be found.
But those who cling to God will be saved
    and receive abundant life
    from the Most High.

They shall not prevail who, in fear,
    seek to destroy the good,
    or with hate
    try to ruin the upright of heart.
These plots will be turned to the good,
    the good of those who live virtuously,
    the good of those who love Yahweh.

People who do evil,
    who seek to kill the poor
    and crush the needy,
    will ultimately fail.

People who maliciously injure the upright
   will inevitably fall.

Our creative God is stronger than all malice.
Yahweh is more powerful
   than any kind of harm.
The Holy One is greater than
   any destruction, even death itself.
God will accomplish every work
   that God desires.
The little that a good person has
   is worth more than all the wealth
   of those who follow evil ways.
Because Yahweh is with
   the upright of spirit,
   they will know true security.
These live in the heart of God.
They shall not be disturbed.

The Holy One sustains all
   who live God's love,
   even when they experience
   many troubles and sorrows.
Though the good person
   may know distress
   their inmost being is held
   in gentle serenity.
Their soul is at peace
   and they will live forever.

But they who do evil know no rest.
All their striving will vanish
   like smoke in the wind.
People who let greed
   dominate their lives
   take much and return nothing.
While those who follow the Holy One
   are generous with all they possess.

Yahweh blesses these generous souls
   with many joys.
Good things quietly flow out to them,
   like water from a never failing spring.

But people who spend their time
   only on their own pleasure,
   who use their talents just for themselves,
   and keep their treasure
   solely for their needs,
   will endure lives like arid deserts
   and have hearts as barren as stones.

Throughout their lives, our God guides
   those who seek God's paths.
Yahweh shows each the way
   that they should go.
The Holy One walks with each of them
   on their particular journey.
If any should stumble and fall,
   this gracious Mystery helps them up,
   for God carefully holds each person
   to bring them safely home.

I have lived a long time
   and now I am old.
I know that nothing can separate
   those who do good
   from the everlasting love of Yahweh.
Therefore turn away from evil
   and do good.
Act justly.
Speak truthfully.
Give generously.
Thus you will know many joys
   in this life
   and you will behold the Most High
   in the life to come.

Do not depart from Yahweh
   and you will live forever.
Even when people do evil
   and try to kill you,
      they will not succeed in destroying you
      for you are held forever
      in the presence of the gracious One.
But the wicked condemn themselves
   by their own choices.
They walk a path to eternal death.
Be patient and wait upon our God.
Though wickedness flourishes for a while,
   it will not prevail.
Yahweh's purposes will be accomplished.
The victory is ultimately God's.

Notice those who do good.
Observe the people who pursue virtue.
They are at peace with themselves
   and they enjoy many blessings.
Yahweh is with people of goodwill.
In times of trouble
   the Most High sustains the upright.

Be patient and wait.
Wait upon the One-Who-Is.
Wait upon the gracious One
   who loves us.

38

Holy One, I am wounded by my sins.
I am weighed down by my wrongdoing.
My offenses are like arrows
   piercing my heart.

I am cut to the depths of my soul.
Knowledge of my misdeeds
    crushes me.
I am sick unto death.
My whole being is diseased.
I am bent over with a burden.
It is a burden too heavy for me to lift.
I am utterly stricken and prostrate.
My mind is distraught and in tumult.
My heart burns in anguish.
I am laid low and groan in sorrow.

Gracious One, all my longings
    are known to you.
You see my repentance.
It is not hidden from you.
I am sick unto death.

Even my friends do not understand.
They pull away from me,
    not knowing what to do,
    while others who know me
    seem glad because of my failures.
These sneer at me
    and make cutting remarks.

I have become like the deaf,
    like one who cannot hear.
I am like a mute,
    like one who cannot speak.
I can not accept affection from my family.
I am deaf to the concern of my friends.
I cannot answer others' taunts and jeers.

Great God, I confess my sins
    and reject them with all my heart.
They fill me with disgust.
I am utterly appalled
    and bent to the ground.

There is nowhere to turn
   but to you, my God.
I turn away from all my sins
   and mourn my failures.
Let me not be tormented by my guilt.

Gracious One, do not leave me.
Help me now!
Forgive my transgressions and rescue me,
   for you are my savior and my God.

39

I said to myself:
I will examine my actions.
I will guard my thoughts
   and not open my mouth.
I will not say anything to create anxiety.
I will be ever watchful of my tongue
   that I may be secure.

So I kept my silence.
But I only suffered more.
My distress grew worse.
Peace fled my heart.
The more I refused to face my disquiet
   the more troubled I became.

The specter of death haunted my days.
It constantly prowled through my nights.
Then I could not help but ask:
Gracious God, how long will I live?
Tell me, what is the measure of my days?
When will my life end?

I know how fleeting our lives are,
    how quickly our days pass us by,
    how soon our time has slipped away.
Our lives are but a few moments.
We are like a flicker of a lightning bug
    seen on a warm summer's eve.

We are no more than a puff of wind,
    or a ripple on a pond,
    or the shadow cast by a leaf
    as it falls to the ground.
The span of our existence is no more
    than the flash of a meteor across the sky.
We are less than a dust mote
    in the plan of creation.
This situation is true
    for every living creature.

People struggle and suffer so much.
They sweat and strain to heap up goods
    and then another inherits them.

Holy One, what can I hope for?
For what do I wait?
Great God, I wait for you.
Gracious One, I put my trust in you.
Save me from my fears.
Deliver me from this dread.

I said to myself:
I will be quiet and I will wait.
I said to Yahweh: I put my hope in you.
Yet I am worn down with my distress.
Death comes as a tidal wave,
    suddenly drowning the land.
It is a tornado, ripping away
    everything held dear.

Gracious Yahweh,
    remove this burden from me.
Listen to my cry and be not far from me.
Grant peace to my heart
    and courage to my trembling soul.

Like my ancestors, I am but a few breaths.
I am but a cloud's fleeting shadow
    on the ground.
Be with me each passing day
    and meet me with mercy
    at the moment of my death.

40

Yahweh, I waited patiently for you.
I looked for you in the midst of my woes.
I trusted you and you rescued me.
You drew me from the tumult.

You lifted me from the miry bog
    which sought to drag me down.
You set my feet on solid ground
    and made my steps secure.

Now I sing a new song of thanksgiving.
I sing a melody of praise and gratitude.
I proclaim the saving kindness
    you have shown to me.
Others too will hear and understand
    the wonder of your care.

Great God, happy are they
    who put their trust in you.

How blessed are they
    who do not put their security
    in the things of this world.
How contented are they
    who do not worship money or power,
    or make a god of their belly.

Holy One, you give
    so many good things.
You multiply blessings
    and shower them upon us.
There is none like you!

Your generous deeds
    are too many to number.
Like the stars in the sky,
    we cannot count them all.
If I tried to name each of them
I would never finish speaking.

Great God, you do not want
    long, sonorous prayers.
You are not interested in offerings
    of silver or gold.
You do not desire the killing of creatures
    to take away sins.
Rather, you long for ears that listen to you.
You look for hearts that love your ways.

Great God, you gave me ears
    that heard your call.
You blessed me with a heart
    that desired your paths.
So I answered: Here I am.
And you taught me in my inmost being.

How I love you, O my God.
My delight is in your will.

Your desires are written
   in my deepest self.

I do not keep the news
   of your infinite love
locked up in my heart.
I am not silent about your mercy
   and your faithfulness.

I have not concealed
   your steadfast care.
Your loyalty never ends
   and love never ceases.
Let your enduring care
   be seen by all generations.
And, Holy One, do not withhold
   your mercy from me.

I tell the good news
   of your kindness
   in the assembly of your people.
You know I will never stop proclaiming
   the wonder of your saving grace.

But many problems
   continue to plague me.
My sins remain
   a constant stumbling block.
My faults and frailties
   at times overwhelm me.
My failures are without number.
They total more than the number
   of hairs on my head or stars in the sky.
I behold this, and again my heart sinks.
My courage slips to nothing.

Yahweh, save me
   as I again slide into despair.

Once more I call out to you:
Make haste to help me!
I rely on you alone.

May those who search for you
   discover you.
May those who are lost in sin
   turn to you and be saved.
May those who are hurting
   find healing and new life.
Then all shall know your greatness
   and sing your praises.

As for me, foolish and weak as I am,
I know you do not cease to love me.
You are my savior and my God.
Come quickly to my aid!

41

Great and gracious One,
   we trust in you.
We trust you in the midst of woe.
We trust you to protect
   and sustain us.
We know you delight in the people
   who spend their lives helping others.

You are close to the poor and oppressed.
You bless those who serve the helpless.
These are the people
   who are especially dear to you.
You surround the compassionate
   with your care.
You lead them in integrity and peace.

O happy are all who follow your ways.
You help them in sickness.
You are with them in every trouble.
You never abandon them.

Holy One, you know our faults
    and you know our sins.
You know how we fail you,
    again and again.
Be merciful to all of us sinners.
Forgive our transgressions
    and heal our failures.
Touch our minds and hearts
    with your renewing spirit.
Touch our bodies too
    with your restoring power.

Still, great God, we feel afraid.
We fear you have deserted us.
We feel you have abandoned us
    because of our sins and our failures.

Even our friends stay away.
They do not visit or come near.
They do not know what to do.
They do not know what to say.
Others, whom we thought were friends,
    have turned against us.
These speak false words.
They heap contempt on us.
They whisper scandal about us
    and picture the worst.

Gracious One, be merciful!
Heal our minds and hearts.
Grant us health of mind and body.
Restore respect to us.
You are truly gentle and kind.

You know we want to be
   your faithful servants.
You have called us your beloved
   and you dignify us by naming us
   your co-workers and friends.

You exalt us by asking us
   to help you in caring for others.
You glorify us by calling us to partner you
   in loving service to our hurting world.
You will help us because you love us.
You have shown us your love
   through your acceptance and support.
Draw us ever closer to yourself.
Keep us in your presence forever.
May all hearts reverence you,
   rejoice in you, and love you,
   for all eternity.

42

As a blind person longs to see,
   or an exile dreams of home,
   so I hunger for you, O God.
As a prisoner yearns for freedom,
   or a lonely person
   thirsts for companionship,
   so I pine for you, my God.
I desire you with all my being.

Holy and loving One,
   where can I go to find you?
Where do I look to behold your face?
What must I do, to again know
   your radiant presence?

Day and night
    my spirit cries out for you.
My body, too, aches
    with poignant longing.

While all around me
people chatter and laugh.
They get and spend.
They eat and sleep.
They rise and walk through their days
    without the stubborn stiletto
    of this desire in their inmost hearts.

And if they knew my anguish,
    they would only say: Where is this God
    that you do not see or touch?
How stupid of you to be so obsessed.

My heart is torn anew, great God,
    each time I remember you.
I remember the intensity of your goodness.
I recall the sweetness of your love.
I thrill anew with joy
    as I glimpse your beauty;
    and I see the magnificence
    of your wisdom.
I want to sing your impossible,
    improbable, wonderful care
    and shout this glorious truth.

Then why do I hurt so much?
Why am I so troubled?
My God, I trust you.
I hope in you and love you.
I trust that, one day,
    this longing will be satisfied.
I hope that one day, I will live
    fully and completely in your presence.

Yet in this exile,
   my heart remains broken.
So once more my whole being
   turns to you.
Waves of longing wash through me.
The anguish of immense desire
   pours over me like the high tide
   upon the shore.

O Holy One, be my strength
   in the midst of this pain.
Grant a love that will meet
   and embrace your coming
   with the same fierceness
   and tenderness
   of your own fiery care.

Still, at times I wonder:
Am I totally crazy?
Have I gone too far?
Have I have lost touch with reality?

While all around me
   people chatter and laugh.
They get and spend.
They eat and sleep.
They sit or saunter along
   their own life's way.
And if they knew my anguish,
   they would only say: Where is this God
   that you do not see or touch?
How stupid of you to be so obsessed.

Holy One, to you I say:
Help me to know your presence
   and walk your path of love.
Help me to follow your way
   of service with all my heart.

Great God, you are my source.
You are my life and my only goal.
You are my dearest hope and help.
You are the heart of my heart.

Gracious One, provide the way
   and create the means
   to faithfully follow you.
Root me ever more deeply
   in the reality of you.
Beloved One, support me
   in this wonderful folly.
Keep me faithful to you
   in this glorious distress.

So why am I so filled with this yearning?
Why am I so troubled by this pain?
I trust and hope in You-Who-Are.
Again I feel such longing and hope.
I long for the day I will rejoice with you
   in your living presence.
I hope for the time I will delight in you
   with all your creation.

43

O Holy One, help us,
   for you are our God.
O gracious One, save us,
   for we have such need of you.

Save us from the material things
   that ensnare us.
Protect us from the attitudes
   that pervert us.

Shield us from so many ideas
    that lead us astray.
Keep us from deceitful thoughts
    and greedy desires.
Turn us from unjust acts
    and harmful beliefs.
Deliver us from vengeful feelings
    and keep us from sliding
        into the deep darkness of depression.

We take refuge in you.
Rescue us from despair
    even when we are besieged
    by doubt or anger or frustration.
Save us when we are sore tested
    by fear or loss or loneliness.
Keep us from hopelessness,
    yes, even when you seem
        to have abandoned us,
        or seem to be but a figment
        of our imagination.

Send us your light and your truth.
These shall lead us on.
Let your light show us your paths.
Let your truth bring us fully
    into your holy presence

May we know your loving care.
Then we will run
    with exceeding joy
    into your enfolding arms,
    like little children
    when their parents' call.

Then we will fly
    with wondrous gladness
    into your embrace as lovers do
    when they have been long parted.

Then, with exultant hearts,
   we will sing praise to you
   who are our loving God.

Do not be disturbed, O my heart.
Do not be cast down, O my soul.
Yahweh is faithful and we are secure
   even in the midst of many troubles.
Hope in God, for we shall once more
   praise the Holy One
   who is our ever present help and joy.

44

O God, your ways are so mysterious.
We do not understand so many experiences.
We do not comprehend so many events.

Yes, we have heard the stories:
   how you walked with our ancestors;
   how you saved them in times of trouble.

We have been told how you rescued them
   and led them to safety in times of distress.
With your support they escaped
   and were set free.
They were set free from past failures.
They were given new beginnings.
They knew the delight
   of your gracious presence.
They gave you thanks for your tender care.
They accomplished great things.

And so we also trusted in you.
We trusted your kindness.

We placed our hope in you.
We gave thanks for your goodness to us.

But now great adversity
   has come upon us.
Total calamity knocks on our door.
So we ask you, Yahweh:
Have you abandoned us?
Have you left us to be deemed a joke
   and called fools?
Are we only rubbish to be stepped on
   and then thrown away?

Great God, we are taunted and scorned.
We are considered to be of no value.
We are devastated by these taunts.

We come to you, Holy One,
   because we are lost.
We feel alone and helpless.
Have you forgotten us?

We try to follow your way.
We have not forgotten you.
We have not turned our hearts
   away from you.

But still we are broken and despised.
Mockery and scorn pierce us like knives.
Depression weighs us down
   like a great stone upon our hearts.
Darkness surrounds us,
   as if we were trapped in a deep well.
It clutches us like arctic water
   clasps a sinking ship.

Save us! My God, why do you delay?
Rescue us and do not hide from us!

Help us, Holy One,
    before we are destroyed!
Come to our aid
    because of your never-failing love.
We wait for you!

45

I am filled with joy, great God.
My heart is bursting with thanksgiving
    for the gift of your glorious presence.
All day long I jubilantly sing
    in humble gratitude.
I want to shout your praise
    from morning to night.

O that I might really express
    this wondrous exaltation.
O that I might truly convey
    this marvelous delight.
And, dear friend, this miracle
    was your gift to me.
Grace was poured out
    through your kind and truthful words.

Yahweh has always blessed you
    and you are a blessing to me.
You illuminated God's wisdom
    and the gracious One's generosity.
You sliced through my confusion
    and lifted my despair.
Thus you revived the smoldering embers
    of ardent delight in our God.
Once more love became a living flame
    in my heart.

Continue, gracious One,
   to vindicate the truth
   and defend the right.
Overcome the oppression
   of sin in our lives
   and death in our spirits.

Let your love, like sharp arrows,
   pierce our limitations.
Take away our sins
   and forgive our offenses.
Great God, bring us all back to you.
You are the One-Who-Is.

Your gracious goodness endures forever.
Your purpose is justice for all peoples.
Your desire is the reclamation of our world.
Your goal is the transformation
   of our entire universe.

Merciful One, you love what is right
   and abhor what is evil.
You call and choose each of us.
You gift us with your love poured out.
Thus immense joy awaits those
   who are open to your call.
Overflowing fullness of being
   will come to those who follow your way.

Holy One, you are an exquisite perfume,
   enchanting the nose.
You are a melodious song,
   intoxicating the ear.
You are all the colors of the rainbow,
   delighting the eye.
You are a passionate dance,
   lifting the heart.

So, your presence fills my inmost being.
Golden robes and precious jewels
  are only shadow symbols
  of the glory that you are.

Yahweh says: Hear, O people!
Listen to my voice, O nations!
Open your minds to my words
  and your hearts to my love.

Forget the crumbling prizes
  of this world.
Turn away from chasing after them.
Shun those idols of money,
  of power and prestige.
Seek your security in me,
  the living God.

O people, center your heart
  in the gracious One
  and you will have inner peace.
Make Yahweh your whole purpose.
Make our God your whole goal
  and blessings will shower upon you.

You will be like spring rain
  on fertile soil.
You will bring forth a great harvest
  of blessings in due season.
Like guests at a wedding feast
  you will be inebriated with joy.
Like a bride or groom
you will see only beauty.
You will feel only the love
  of your beloved.

Your family will follow in gladness.
Friends and neighbors will rejoice.

They will be led with joy.
They will share
    in Yahweh's abundant life.
Nothing will be lost.

Yahweh, let my song of praise
    celebrate you through all generations.
Let my heartfelt gratitude please you.

May I bring joy to the joyless.
May I be hope to the hopeless
    and may all peoples praise you
    forever and ever.

46

Be still and know that I am God.
I am Who-I-Am.
I am beingness itself,
    bursting forth,
    ever ancient, ever new.
Nothing shakes me
    or overwhelms me.
Nothing defeats the fulfillment
    of my greatest designs
    or smallest desires.

Though the mountains
    wear away to dust
    and the oceans
    turn into barren plains,
    though the universe itself
    should collapse into nothing,
I remain and my love remains,
    constant and secure.
Be still and know that I am God.

Great God, like cool shade
   in the desert heat,
   your presence makes us glad.
Like a warm fire
   on a cold winter's night.
   your presence maintains life
   and brings us joy.
You are in the midst
   of your creation.
All that you love shall endure.

When you speak
   the day of glory dawns.
When you send forth your renewing word
   the earth shakes,
   the nations crumble,
   and the prideful plans of peoples melt away.

Yahweh is the One-Who-Is-With-Us.
Holy One, you are our ever present refuge.
You are the source of our strength.
Come! See what the Holy One has done!
See the marvelous deeds of our God.

Yahweh makes wars to cease
   and violence to be no more.
Weapons of war are totally destroyed.
Violence is banished
   from the human heart
   and peace flourishes
   throughout our world.

Be still and know that I am God.
I am the joy of the nations
   and the glory of all peoples.

You are with us, Holy One.
You are our hope and refuge forever.

47

All you peoples, clap your hands.
Sing to God with songs of gladness,
    for Yahweh is more wonderful
    than we can really comprehend.
The Most High is far deeper
    than our ability to understand.
The wisdom of our God is beyond compare.
The mercy of our God is beyond measure.

Gracious One, you are our God
You are the creator of the universe.
You are the sustainer of all that exists.
You are the source of all good
    and author of all truth.
Great God, you are
    the One-Who-Calls-Us.
You are the One-Who-Chooses-Us.
You always tenderly hold us
    within your everlasting embrace.

O peoples, lift up your hearts with joy
    and shout aloud with exultant praise,
    for nothing can separate us
    from our God's constant love.
As a space satellite circles
    the whole earth as it orbits our planet,
    so from beginning to end our God
    embraces the whole of creation.

Holy One, you are with us.
You are always in our midst.
Yet you soar high above
    our capacity to understand.
You work at depths far beyond
    our level of awareness.

Holy One, you are with us.
You are always in our midst.
You shatter human arrogance
    like a mighty earthquake
    shatters human structures on the earth.

Your presence destroys human malice
    as a tornado destroys everything it touches.
Human greed evaporates in your light
    like dew in the morning sun.
Evil does not survive in your presence.

Yes, Holy One, you are with us.
You are always in our midst.
You are skillfully working
    to build the earth.
You are carefully laboring
    to establish your kin-dom.
All you peoples sing out your praise,
    giving thanks to our most high
    and gracious God.

48

Consider God's greatness.
Yahweh towers above our intellects
    like the snow capped Himalayas
    tower above the continental plain.

Consider God's goodness.
Yahweh's mercy embraces the universe
    like the atmosphere enfolds our planet,
    enabling all life to exist.

Gracious One, you are beauty
    in your absolute beingness.
You are awesome in your splendor.
You are joy in your goodness.
You are light in your truth.
You carefully hold all things
    in your love.

When troubles attack us,
    you are there to calm our fears.
When anxieties oppress us,
    your presence lifts their weight
    and we are free.
When terror stalks our lives,
    you touch our hearts with peace.

Our panic crumbles and flees away.
Holy One, again we ponder
    your steadfast love.
You are in our midst,
    in the midst of your people.
Then, surprisingly, your love leaps up
    like an immense geyser
    lifting our inmost being
    while we dance with joy
    and sing songs of praise.

The wonder of you fills the earth.
Let all your people give you thanks
    because of your abiding care.
Let all your creatures be glad
    because of your enduring concern.

Rest your heart upon
    Yahweh's faithful love.
Meditate upon the Holy One's
    eternal mercy.
Carefully consider God's words
    and works.

Tell your children
    and your children's children
    of God's surpassing kindness.

Yahweh will guide and save us.
Yahweh, our God, is forever and ever.

49

Turn to me, O people!
And listen to me.
Whether you are great or humble,
    whether you are rich or poor,
I speak wisdom
    and my words are clear.
The thoughts of my heart
I place before you.
I will explain the truth of life.

I do not fear in times of trouble.
I am secure when problems besiege me
    or enmity surrounds me.

How foolish are they who trust in riches
    and boast of their great wealth.
They imagine themselves to be secure
    with all their possessions.
Yet they will not live forever.
Though they may purchase
    a few more hours or days of life,
    they can not buy themselves eternity.
Their possessions do not follow them
    into the grave and their riches
    will become the property of others.

Foolish are they who trust in their talents
    and seek the praise of their peers.
They imagine themselves to be secure
    in their reputation and accomplishments.
Yet these are fragile things.
They are easily swept away,
    like leaves in an autumn wind.
A reputation can be broken as quickly
    as glass dropped on pavement.
Accomplishments do not
    save people from death.
Talented people pass away
    just like common folks.

See what happens to those who trust
    only in themselves.
These live as if God did not exist.
They only pursue the paths of their desires
    while they give no thought to eternity.
Though these consider themselves happy
    and are praised for doing well,
    when riches flee and health fails,
    no one cares for them.

When their talents fade and honors depart,
    emptiness is their constant companion.
And when their remaining years are few
    despair hounds their inmost heart.
The grave will be their final home
    and death their eternal inheritance.

O people, listen to me.
Do not depend on riches
    or the accolades of others.
But those who are faithful to Yahweh
    do not fear death.

Consider Yahweh's goodness
    with an open heart.

Be attentive to God's mercy now!
Turn to the Holy One
    who will rescue you.
Follow Yahweh's desires
    and you will be saved.
Yahweh is forever,
    and where God is,
        those who love God will also be.

Therefore shout your joy.
Dance your thanksgiving.
For God, our God, is with us
    and we will be with the Holy One forever.

50

The God of Abraham and Sara speaks:
    the God of Miriam and Moses,
    of Mary and Joseph and Jesus,
    the God who creates and sustains all things,
    this God speaks to the whole world.
Yahweh shines forth in all that is good
    and generates everything
    beautiful and true.
The Holy One calls all creation
    to witness these words.

God comes speaking gently
    to those in need
    and thundering fiercely—in rebuke
    of those who live only for themselves.

Yahweh calls to us, saying:
Hear me my people!
Come to me and listen to my words!

I Am Who I Am,
I Am the God of your hearts.
I Am the One through whom
    all things are made.
I am the One
    in whom all things have their being.
I am your God and I speak the truth.

I do not need your churches and temples.
I take no joy in buildings.
Neither do I need any kind of wealth.
I do not ask for gold or silver.
Gold and silver, platinum and precious gems,
    are as mud and sand to me.
Extravagant processions do not honor me.
I have no need of rituals and feast days.
Neither do I need your fasts
    and prayers of supplication.
Instead, know what you need
    and give what is good.

I created forests and raised mountains.
I established the rivers
    and gathered the oceans into their beds.
I brought forth the birds of the air
    and every beast of the field.
I make all things and all things are mine.

I do not need your praise.
But you need to acknowledge my gifts.
You need to praise me for my goodness
    and give me thanks for blessings
    because I am God,
    and not you, yourselves.

My precious little ones,
    give me thanks with all your heart.
This is the acceptable return I desire.

Open your hearts to the poor.
Console those who are hurting.
This is the praise I seek.
Be patient and kind
    with your brothers and sisters.
Be generous to those in need.
This is the worship that pleases me.

Place your trust in me
    and I will be with you.
Call upon me in your struggles
    and I will walk with you.
I, myself, will lead you
    through every trouble into New Life.

You will find rest for your hearts
    and dance in my presence
    with joyful gratitude,
    for I am your God,
    and not you, yourselves.

I also speak to those who ignore me
    and to the ones
    who close their ears to my call.
I admonish the people
    who mock me,
    and reprove the ones who say:
There is no God.
I reprimand the ones
    who take no thought of me.

I say to those who follow after sin:
I abhor your speaking evil
    and telling lies.
I detest your fault-finding
    and your violence.
I abominate your oppression
    of even the least
    of your brothers and sisters.

Your self-centered, self-seeking lives
   will end in your annihilation.
No matter how impressive
   you think your lives are to others,
   they are nothing to me.

Listen to me, all of you
   who ignore my words.
You court destruction.
Turn to me and follow my way!

A grateful heart is a joy to me.
A generous spirit honors me.
I will surely save all who obey me,
   for I am your God,
I am the One-Who-Is-With-You always.

51

O God, be merciful to me
   because you are steadfast love.
My God, have pity on me
   out of your infinite kindness.
Wipe away my transgressions
   and wash away all my sins.
Cleanse me from every failure.

O God, my many sins are before me.
I see my frequent failures.
So often I turned away from you
   and followed corrupt desires.
I voiced ideas and carried out actions
   that hurt others and myself.
Thus I have sinned against you.

I hurt you as well as others,
   because you identify yourself
   with even the lowest part
   of your creation.

Holy One, I have no defense.
I can offer no excuse.
There is no way to justify myself.
You can rightfully chastise me.
Condemnation is fitting
   and punishment is proper.
Because of my heedless self-seeking,
I cared nothing for the effect
   of my actions on anyone or anything.

Since I was a child, I was concerned
   solely with advancing my desires.
In my youth, my ideas were often wrong
   and my actions were frequently contrary
   to your commands.
Holy One, you desire truth
   with others and ourselves.
You demand honesty before you.
You want truth in thought
   and honesty in action.

Therefore teach me you wisdom
   and let me know your forgiveness.
Keep me honest to the depths
   of my mind and heart.
Remove my sins and I shall be clean.
Purify me and I shall be
   whiter than snow.
Wash me and I shall know
   freedom and peace.

Let me hear once more the sounds of joy.
Let me feel again an awareness of gladness.

Then, though I am crushed by anguish
   or broken in distress, I will rejoice anew
   because you have forgotten my sins
   and wiped away my failures.

O God, create in me a new heart
   and put your faithful spirit within me.
Do not turn away from me.
Do not take your Holy Spirit from me.

Restore me to the joy
   of your loving presence.
Keep me steadfast in your ways
   of truth and life.
Help me to teach others of your mercy.
Then sinners will turn back to you.

Gracious One, deliver me
   from vainglory.
Save me from despair.
How gladly I will proclaim
   your goodness.
Let me speak of your love
   and declare your mercy.

You do not desire external sacrifices.
You are not pleased
   with pretentious gestures.
My offering, O God, is a humble spirit.
I really want to do your will.
I sincerely wish to follow your way.
You will not reject a humble heart.
You will not spurn a contrite spirit.

Holy One, continue to bless our world.
Touch and turn all people to you.
Help us to build
   your kin-dom among us.

Then we will worship you
   with loving gratitude
   as we proclaim your gracious goodness
   among the nations.

52

O great and gracious God, so often
   the wicked of this world like to boast.
They tell of their devious exploits
   with immense relish.
They plot the ruin of others
   and invent lies to foster their selfish ambitions.
They avidly pursue riches and power.
They think this world belongs to them.

As a wave flows out from a moving ship,
   so insult and injury flow out
   from their treacheries.
They heap scorn on the vulnerable
   and injustice on the poor.
They seek to destroy anything
   that stands in the way of their desires.

But you, great God, are faithful and eternal.
You will not be patient forever.
You will snatch from their homes
   the people who do evil.
You will uproot them from the land
   of the living.
Their treacherous deeds
   lead to nothing but dust.
Their lying tongues will be silenced.
All that they are and all that they own
will crumble away to be no more.

This is not what will happen
    to those who seek your will.
Your faithful people may never know
    earthly power or wealth or fame,
    but they will be secure.

Your people find refuge in you.
They are consoled by your abiding love.
They are safe in your tender embrace.
These are like large, green trees
    which provide shade for the weary.
They are like groves of fruit trees
    that provide food for the hungry
    at harvest time.

Your people trust your mercy
    and rejoice in your wisdom.

They thank you for your blessings
    and praise you for your steadfast love.
They are at peace
    even in the midst of woe.

O Holy One, I will declare
    your faithfulness among the peoples.
I will proclaim your goodness
because of all the wonders you have done.

Blessed be you, most gracious One,
    forever and ever.

53

This world swarms with people
   who know only despair.
Our streets are full of the walking dead.
Those who have no faith see nothing ahead.
Thus they spend their lives seeking after
   new pleasures and excitements.
But they also yearn for security
   and contentment.

Eventually and inevitably, their experience
   becomes that of total boredom.
These people lose all hope
   that anything will give them
   lasting pleasure or peace.
Chronic discontent, anxiety,
   cynicism, and despondancy follow.
The self-centered destroy themselves.
Their way is corrupt
   and their actions abominable.

Yahweh, you see the heart
   of every person.
You look for people who seek you.
You pursue each person
   so all may know you.
You seek everyone
   so that each may experience
   your love for them
   and rest securely in your care.
Yet so many refuse.
They turn away.

Great God, we all fail to live
   your greatest hopes for us.

We do not pursue
　　your finest dreams for us.
There is no one
　　who does not trip and fall into sin.
There is not one
　　who fully lives your plan
　　for their good.

And those who are lost in sin
　　have no knowledge of your goodness.
They wreak havoc on this world.
They heap pain and sorrow
　　upon all in their path.

Merciful One, how little we know.
How great is our need.
You who are the living God,
　　turn our hearts to you.
You who can raise the dead,
　　raise us to life in you.
You who are fullness and joy,
　　fill our emptiness with your plenitude—
　　pressed down, shaken together,
　　and running over.
So, Holy One, we ask
　　your deliverance for all of us.

O that you would touch
　　and turn and transform us.
Bring fullness to our emptiness
　　and life from our deadness.
Then our hearts will rejoice
　　and our spirits will be glad.
Then all people will break forth
　　in songs of gratitude to you-who-are forever.

54

Yahweh, help us!
Gracious One, hear our prayer!
Everything has gone wrong.
Nothing works and nothing is right.
Nothing makes sense in our lives.
We feel abandoned and afraid.
Yahweh, where are you? Help us!

The insolent, the ruthless,
    and the depraved show no fear.
They lie and cheat with audacity.
They steal with impunity.
They have no thought for you.
They have no care but for themselves.

These people devastate our world.
They crush us brutally.
Daily they beat us down.
Daily they assault and annihilate us.
They get away with murder
    and nothing stops them.
Yahweh, surely you will help us.
You will vindicate your people.
You will not allow the impious
    to destroy your faithful little ones.
In your steadfast love,
    you will show us the way.
You will restore our lives
    and repair our world.

Then, how joyfully we will sing your praise.
We will thank you with all our hearts
    for you are good
    and you deliver us from every evil.

55

Merciful God, we are such needy souls.
So from the depths of my need
I cry out to you.
Gracious One, listen to me!
I am worn out with worry.
I am anxious and empty.

Anger and confusion fill my days.
Fear and dread haunt my nights.
It seems like death stands at my door.
I am gripped by terror
  and overcome by weariness.

O that I had wings like a bird.
I would fly away and find rest.
I would flee to the ends of the earth.
I would soar swiftly to a safe shelter
  far from the raging winds of misfortune.

O God, take away my fear.
Calm the storm in my heart.
I see violence everywhere.
Wrongdoing surrounds me.
Despair enfolds me
  and disaster looms over me
  like a thunderhead.

Fraud and depravity are everywhere.
If I could blame another,
I could endure it.
If it was someone else,
I could hide from them.
But I am the source of my woes.
How can I run from myself?

Great God, I call upon you for help.
Morning, noon, and night
I cry out to you: Save me, Holy One!
Hear my lament and answer my need.
Surely you will bring me to safety.
You who hold the universe
    in the palm of your hand
    will touch my heart and heal me,
    for you are my God.

When I am angry,
    calm my mind and heart.
When I am confused,
    grant me understanding.
When I am fearful, soothe my alarm.
When I am crushed and defeated,
    lift my heart with new hope.
When I am sad and lonely,
    anoint me again with the oil of gladness.

O people, cast your troubles
    on the One-Who-Is
    the one who is with you and for you.
The Holy One is ever near.
God is faithful and will keep you close.
Yahweh's peace will enfold you
    and God's mercy will heal you.
Gracious God, I do trust in you!

56

Gracious God, hear my plea.
I pour out my anger
    and speak my unhappiness.
I will not hide my anxiety from you.

Holy One, I try to please you.
I have listened to your word.
I have tried to follow your way,
    the way you want me to live.
But peace eludes me
    and prosperity is an illusion.

I believe in you and trust you.
I reverence you with all my heart.
Yet troubles surround me
and more misery approaches.

Why can't you come to me?
Why don't you provide for my needs?
Why isn't there just a little
    of the rapture that was once between us?

O the joy that inundated me
    and the strength that upheld me.
O the confidence that filled me
    and the peace that surrounded me.

O the radiant ecstasy
    of your loving presence near me.
O your tender touch
    that flowed through me
    to embrace everyone with ardent concern
    and everything with heartfelt gratitude.

Be gracious to me, most Holy One.
Do not let my anger overwhelm me.
Do not let my frustration cause me to fall.
Do not let my fear turn into flight from you.

O Most High, when I am angry,
    help me to put my trust in you.
When I am frustrated, let me praise you.
When fear grips me, turn me toward you.

I will look to you in dark surrender,
   for the gates of hell
      will not prevail against you.

Yet daily, obstacles constrict me
   and worries pour in on me.
Black thoughts frequent my days.
They stir up images of misery.
I am sickened by forebodings of disaster.
Nightmares fill my nights with images
   of wrath, discouragement, and dismay.

Gracious One, you know my sorrow.
I do not hide my tears from you.
My troubled heart I give to you
   for I believe in your love for me.
I believe that, at your word,
   all these problems will be lifted.

You are the God in whom I trust.
You are the One whom I praise.
You are Who-You-Are and I am not afraid
   for these sorrows will end
   and all troubles will pass away
   like mist on a summer morn.

Great God, I will keep
   my promises to you.
I trust you completely
   and worship you with all my being.
You deliver me from death.
You keep me from falling into sin
   and stumbling into despair.

So, great and gracious God,
I will walk in your presence.
And, though the light of your presence
   continues as darkness for me,

I know your light will yet shine
   on all the living.

So I will praise you,
Most High and Holy One,
   all the days of my life.

57

Be merciful to me!
O God, be merciful to me!
I come to you for protection.
I seek refuge in the your loving presence,
   until this raging storm passes by.

I look to you, Most High.
I look to you with hope.
You will complete your purposes.
You will save me.
You will lift me from my troubles.
You will surround me
   with your enduring love.

These are distressing times.
Wars and violence abound.
Famine and death stalk this earth.
My heart is torn by the travail of peoples.
I am pierced by their pain.
I am overwhelmed by their suffering.

Holy One, show forth your greatness.
Manifest your goodness.
Let your forgiveness fill the earth.

Let your mercy drop down
    like gentle spring showers
    which soften the earth.
Let your love break forth anew,
    like a flood of life-giving water
    bringing new growth to thirsty ground.

Though the peoples are beleaguered
    and bowed down with distress,
    in the end
    those who persecute your little ones
    only destroy themselves.

Great God, my hope in you is steadfast.
Holy One, my hope is only in you.
My confidence in you is unshaken.
My trust is absolute.

A song of joy awakens in my soul.
I sing in gratitude all the day.
In my heart is a glorious melody.
I will awaken the dawn with my praise.

I will give thanks to you
    among all the peoples.
I will adore you among the nations.
Your ardent love is deeper
    than the depths of the universe itself
    and your faithfulness
    reaches to the ends of time.

Gracious One, reveal your greatness.
Holy One, disclose your goodness.
Let your forgiveness cover our world
    and your mercy endure forever.

58

Yahweh, so many people think only
   of pursuing their own desires.
Many more seek only
   their own pleasures.
These people heap up injustices.
They lie and cheat and manipulate
   to gain their own ends.
They who think of themselves alone
   commit all kinds of violence.

The whole social order is corrupted.
From birth to death, evils surround us.
Like a deadly poison
   in the very fabric of our lives,
   envy and deceit pollute,
   pride distorts,
   greed and anger pervert,
   lust and sloth debase,
   and fear rules our hearts.

O God, cure us from these mortal evils.
Set us free from violence and fear.
Drain the poison of lies and manipulation.
Dissolve corruption and abolish evil.
Turn fear to faith and despair to hope.
Draw us all to yourself,
   so we may be transformed
   and made anew.

You are the final word, O God.
Your judgments are true
   and your fidelity is forever.
We look to you for that final word
   and for the vindication of those
   who suffer injustice of any kind.

Great God, happy are they who turn to you.
Happy are they who trust you,
    for you are the One who judges the world.
You judge the world with truth.
You judge the peoples with equity.

Then all your little ones will shout:
Praise God!
They will sing: Blessed be Yahweh!
Blessed be the God who is with us.
Blessed be the One who is for us.
Blessed be Yahweh,
    the One who saves us forever and ever.

59

Come, great God, and rescue me.
Save me from everything
that separates me from you.
Rescue me from all that is harmful.
Deliver me from the evil that others do.

All day long I am battered by confusions
    and surrounded by conflicts.
All night long, I am assailed by doubts
    and tormented by fears.

Malice prowls like a lion
    waiting to attack.
Calumny slinks like a jackal
    seeking to rend and tear.
Deliver me, O God, from unjust attacks
    and defend me from vicious lies.

Words, like sharp knives,
    are thrown at me.
Hostility, like a thick fog,
    swirls around me.
But you, great God,
know the whole of it.
Nothing is hidden from you.

O my strength, I look to you.
O my courage, I call upon you
    for you are my God.
Let your never-failing love protect me.
With your infinite care, be with me.
Through your mercy, save me.

Turn the calumny to dust.
Bring the malice to nothingness.
Let justice rule and goodness prevail.
Then all the peoples will know
    your wisdom and strength.
They will see your faithful love.

Gracious One, again I say:
Save me from the lion.
Defend me from the jackal.
Though they prowl,
they will find no prey.

So I will sing of your loving kindness.
I will proclaim your steadfast care.
For you are my constancy and courage
    through all tribulations.

O my Fidelity, I sing your praise.
O my Courage, I declare your love,
    for you are the One who upholds me.

You shower your mercies
    on every generation.

Great God, all the earth
    shall see your goodness.
Let all who live in our world
    see your mercy.

Holy and gracious God,
    you have made us and you know us.
You also know this world is dense with evil.

This planet is overflowing
    with our injustices.
The soil itself cries out from our harm
    and the oceans suffer desperately
    because of our rampant misuse.

The peoples suffer too.
They are stalked by destruction.
Disease is a needless companion
    for too many souls.
Hunger is the daily bedmate
    for so many more.

Holy One, you have given us warning.
You have shown us what we need to do
    so we may live and prosper.
This world is the work of your hand.
We are to be careful conservators
    of this planet.
We are to use its resources for the good,
    for the good of everything that lives.
All peoples are our brothers and sisters.
We are to care for each other as one family.

You have promised
   to be with us and to help us.
You are faithful to your promises.
You will lead us to live in peace.
You will help us to seek justice
   for everyone.

O gracious One, grant us your wisdom
   so we may grow in understanding.
Grant us your Spirit
   so we may grow in compassion.
Our minds are too limited.
Our wills too weak
   and the situations too complex
   for ourselves alone to solve.

Generous One, with your help
   goodness will prevail
   and evil will be no more.
Merciful One, you will provide
   and justice shall be established
   over all the earth.
Great God, hear our prayer
   and answer our need!

61

Gracious God, I call out to you.
Holy One, listen to my prayer.
I am at my wits' end.
I am at the limit of my endurance.

My hope in you is but a faint shadow
   in my soul.

My trust in you is but a whisper
    in my heart.
Touch me with the power of your Spirit
    for you are my only refuge.

You are the One-Who-Abides with all.
You are the One-Who-Leads each of us.
Support me now, in this hour of need.
Keep me close to you in every moment.
Hide me in the shelter of your love.

Yahweh, you heard my promises to you.
You are my life, my light, and my joy.
You are my heritage forever.

Bring forth years of peace
    in this troubled world.
Let our hearts be graced with wisdom.
Let our spirits expand with generosity.
May forgiveness rule our minds
    and compassion be the foundation
    of our lives.

Let abiding love be our compass
    and faithfulness be our guide.
May we overflow with gratitude
    and be filled with trust.

Thus we will fulfill your desires for us
    and praise you with pure hearts
    all the days of our lives.

62

Yahweh, my God, I wait for you alone.
I wait patiently for your word to me.
With expectant heart I seek you
    for you are my only hope.

You are my safe haven
    and my salvation.
You will finish the work
    that you have begun in me.
You will complete your purposes
    for our world.

When I am battered by circumstances,
    when I am as weak as a baby
    or as tottering as a sick old person,
    when others attack my ideas
    and cast contempt on my ideals,
I turn to you who are my refuge.
I seek you who are my hope.

Gracious One, I wait for you alone.
I search for you with desperate longing.
You alone are my life and my joy.
You are my source of strength and courage.
You will complete your work in me.

The troubles of this world
    are like a passing gust of wind.
They are like the moving shadows
    of clouds upon the ground.

O people, trust in our faithful God.
Pour out your heart
    before the One-Who-Is.
The Holy One is our refuge.

This merciful One is our strength.
Yahweh is our rock and our salvation.

In the end, we all die.
When we are gone,
    this earth sees us no more.
Therefore, put no confidence in things.
Money will not save us
    from sorrow or death.
Power slips away with time
    and fame is fleeting.
An admirable reputation
    may be as as fickle as the wind.
Intelligence fades into senility.

Hope in any of these is vain.
Do not set your desire on them.

Yahweh has spoken.
The meaning of each life
    is hidden in God's heart.
The mystery of death
    is known by God alone.

Holy One, steadfast love
    belongs only to you.
You, the One-Who-Is,
    are the very gift which you give.
And you give immeasurably
    from your infinitely steadfast love.
Gracious One, bring us all
    safely home to you.

63

Holy One, you are my God.
Earnestly I seek you.
My whole soul thirsts for you
   like a desert traveler yearns for water.
My whole soul is drawn to you
   like iron filings are pulled toward a magnet.
My whole heart yearns for you
   like long separated lovers
   ache for each other.

Let me see you in every moment.
Let me know your presence
   in every circumstance.
Let me ponder the splendor of you
   for you are my wisdom and delight.

You are Who-You-Are.
Your abiding love is better than life.
So I will rejoice in your gracious goodness
   and I will give you thanks
   for your wonderful care.
As with a rich feast, you satisfy my soul.
I will pour out my gratitude
   for all your mercies.
I will lift my heart in joy.
I will sing praise to You-Who-Are
   everyday of my life.

I remember you at night
   when I lay in my bed.
I think of you with love
   for you have always been my solace.
You are my wisdom and courage.
You are my truth and justice.
You are my all, in all.

In the shadow of your presence,
I shout with overflowing happiness.
My soul clings to you and you support me.
With tender strength you uphold me.
No trouble shall overwhelm me.
No sorrow shall destroy me
   and no power on earth
     can separate me from You-Who-Are.

Blessed be you, most gracious One,
   forever and ever.

64

O God, I am so very anxious
   and dread overwhelms me.
Great God, listen to me!
Gracious One, I am so very frightened.
Hear my cry and rescue me.
Preserve my hope
   in the midst of this turmoil.
Keep me from sin
   and shield me from evil.
Protect me from unsuspected traps.
Save me from unruly passions.
Shield me from spite and arrogance,
   and the injury of cruel words.
Shelter me from shameless lies
   that cut me to the bone.
Defend me from slander
   which is like filth
   that is viciously thrown at me.

The human heart is a deep enigma.
A person's thoughts are often hidden.

But you, great God, know everything.
When someone does evil, you know it.
When another thinks wickedness, you see it.
When people harbor malice in their hearts and say
    "No one can see our intent,"
    they are wrong,
    because their purpose stands out clearly
    before you.

When foolish people
    encourage each other to follow evil ways,
    they talk about their intrigues,
    saying: This is a perfect scheme.
Great God, you are there and know it all.

Evil designs will ultimately fail.
Foul plots will fall to ruin.
Treacherous plans will collapse
    and those who hatch them will be trapped
    in the web of their own machinations.
People around them will see their ruin
    and be amazed.

Holy One, your little ones will see this
    and be happy.
These will recognize it as your work.
They will think about your saving kindness.
They will declare your acts of grace
    and proclaim your deeds of power.

Happy are all who trust in you.
These people are eternally secure
    in your gracious love.
No antagonism will disturb
    their inner peace.
No evil can overwhelm them.
Rejoicing, they will praise you forever.

65

Generous God,
  it is right for us to praise you.
It is proper to turn to you with gratitude.
It is fitting to give you thanks.
Because you are the One
  who answers our prayers.
We will keep our promises to you
  and perform the vows we have made
  in the assembly of your people.

Happy are the people who come to you.
Blessed are all who turn to you
  with humble and contrite hearts.
They shall find welcome
  in your tender embrace.
You greet them with great joy
  and fill them with good things.
They shall be completely fulfilled.
They shall be totally satisfied.
Nothing shall disturb
  their tranquility of spirit.

All humanity shall come to you.
They will receive your mercy
  and see your love.
You will forgive all our sins.
You will blot out all our transgressions.
And when our faults defeat us,
  you will overlook them too.

Holy One, your gentle goodness
  fills our days with joy.
You are the God of our salvation.
You are the hope of your people
  over all the earth.

Even those across the farthest seas
  shall see and trust in you.

You established this planet
  and set the stars in their orbits.
You raised up the mountains
  and restrained the roaring sea.
You calm the tumult among the peoples.
You quell the clamor of violence
  and the outrage of war.
You have kept us in peace.

The whole world is awed
  by your deeds.
The peoples gawk in wonder
  at your works.
Your great acts bring shouts of joy.
Cries of gladness come
  from the ends of the earth.
From morning to night, your peoples
  sing their songs of praise to you.

Gracious One, you show
  your constant care for this world.
Rain and sun are your gift to all.
You send the rain and water the soil.
It becomes richly fertile.
Streams are filled and rivers flow,
  providing abundant food for the peoples.

You bless the land with sun
  and foster the growth of crops.
You restrain cold and flood.
You withhold drought and keep insects
  from destroying the harvest.
The year is crowned with a bountiful yield.
There is plenty for everyone.

Flocks and herds cover the hills.
The pastures overflow with sheep
and meadows are dotted with cattle.
The land is decked in flowers
and the plains clothed in grasses.

Even the barren lands are awash
with riotous life
and the desert places are filled
with abundant growth.
Wheat and rice, corn and beans,
fill the valleys.
All creation sings for joy.

Praise to the Holy One who is.
Blessed be Yahweh who has done this.
Blessed be our creator and sustainer,
Blessed be this marvelous mystery,
our rescuer and sanctifier forever.

66

Shout joyfully to God, all the earth.
Sing the wonders of Yahweh.
Give the Holy One glory and praise.
Say to God:
How awesome your deeds;
how wonderful your ways.
For you come to deliver
and not to punish,
to raise up and not to crush.

The earth gloriously blooms
with your generosity.

The peoples bow in wonder
   at your mercy.
All the nations worship you
   with grateful hearts.

Remember what God did in the past.
Look and see
   what Yahweh is doing now.
Confidently expect
   what God will do for you.

Holy One, over and over
   you come to us.
Over and over you do not abandon us.
Rather, you patiently invite us
   to come back to you.
Despite our rebellions,
   you invite us to return.
Through our failures and sins,
   you wait for us.
When we complain to you,
   you listen to us.
And when we are fearful,
   you comfort us.

Gracious One, when we turn to you
   with contrite hearts,
   you forgive us and you make us new.
How deep is your wisdom, merciful One.
How patient and understanding you are.

Bless our God, all you peoples.
Let grateful praise be heard.
For our God wants us to live.
Our God wants us to love.
Our God gives us God's own love
   and pours out compassion on all peoples.

So when we are filled with anguish,
    when harsh and dreadful events occur,
    or terrible things come into our lives,
    when violence surrounds us
    or anger washes over us
    when we stagger with pain
    or fall under impossible burdens,
Yahweh is with us.

Gracious One, you are our ultimate good.
As we wait in simple hope
    in the barren darkness of our hearts,
    we look for the good
    you will somehow create.
We await the fulfillment of your promise
    when at last you will bring us home
    to live with you forever.

Our God experiences our anguish.
Yahweh feels our sorrow.
When we seek for Yahweh in our pain,
God touches us with redemptive peace.

Holy One, once again
    we will come to your house
    with overflowing joy.
We will sing our wonder
    in praise of Who-You-Are.
How great you are!
O God, how great you are!

So, most gracious One,
    we turn to you in praise.
We give you thanks
    for your great goodness.
We give you our hearts.
We give you our lives.
We give you our very selves,
    in gratitude and love.

You continue to be with us
    through all our troubles.
You hear our bitter cries
    in every affliction.
You bring us back to life with you
    when we have gone astray.

Come and hear,
    all of you who seek meaning in life!
Listen to me, all of you
    who are crushed and desolate!
I will tell you what Yahweh has done.

I turned to God for help
    and this gracious Mystery was there.
God helped me in spite of my sins.
Yahweh helped me in spite of failures.

I asked Yahweh to stay with me.
I asked the Holy One to lead me.
I asked God to give me what I needed
    and Yahweh touched me with courage.
The gracious One gave me new insights
    and filled me with peace.
Indeed, Yahweh listened and provided
    what was truly good for me.

Blessed be the Holy One
    who rejects no one.
Blessed be Yahweh,
    for God hears our cries.
Our God's steadfast love does not cease.
Blessed be the Holy One forever!

67

Glorious and compassionate God,
May you be merciful and bless us.
May you look with favor on us.
May your love be known over all the earth
   and your salvation spread over all nations.

O gracious One, let the peoples praise you.
Let all the peoples praise you.
Let the nations be glad and sing for joy
   for you are a just and merciful judge.

You reach out to the whole human family
   with your wisdom
   and judge everyone with equity.
You work for justice among the peoples.
You impartially do good for every nation.

Great God, let all the peoples praise you.
Let all the nations praise you.
Let your word be the guide of the peoples
and your will be the desire of the nations.

The earth yields a rich harvest.
Yahweh, our God, blesses us.
May all peoples be blessed.
May the peoples of the earth revere you
   and all nations, everywhere, honor you
   who are our eternal living God.

68

Yahweh comes
  and wickedness is exposed.
Iniquity is blown away
  like smoke in the wind.
Malice too disappears in a flash
  and violence shrivels, turning to dust.
Dishonesty melts away
  like the morning mist.
No evil can exist in Yahweh's presence.

But they who seek God shall rejoice.
They who love God's ways
  shall be radiant with gladness.
They shall exult exceedingly
  before the Holy One-Who-Is.
Let all who love Yahweh shout for joy.

Sing your praise to our gracious God.
Pour out your songs to the One-Who-Is.
Yahweh is Fullness-of-Being.
Yahweh is beingness itself:
  beingness overflowing.
Yahweh encompasses all creation.
O sing praise and exult before our God.

Yahweh embraces the forsaken
  and protects the helpless.
Yahweh consoles the sorrowing
  and welcomes the stranger.
Yahweh leads prisoners to freedom
  and proclaims reconciliation to sinners.
Our God is a God of steadfast love.

O God, you are always reaching out
  to each person and all peoples.

You search for the lost
   and bind up the wounded.
You heal the sick and reclaim the sinner.
Nothing is impossible for you.
You will lead all humanity to truth and life.

The earth quakes with your coming.
The skies open and stars fall
   when you draw near.
Yet you are also found in silence
   and in the still small voice
   within each soul.

Great God, you are the source
   of all existence.
You give life to every creature.
You provide for all our needs.
You restore us when we languish.
We are secure in your care.
You take great joy
   in your faithful little ones.

Holy One, those who worship power
   will try to flee from you.
Those who practice violence
   will seek to hide from you.
A person filled with greed
   can not find you.
They who grasp at money
   or connive for status
   are like leaky boats that drift aimlessly
   upon the open sea.

Where are the powerful
   of history now?
Where is the fame of so many
   who have gone down to dust?
They are remembered no more.

Where are they who used
    and abused others?
Where are the violent and malicious,
    as well as the arrogant
    and the malcontent?
Their place sees them no more.
But God is forever.

Yahweh despises violence
    and hates selfishness.
Those who use and abuse others
    cut themselves off from life.
Yet God does not cease to care
    even for these.

Blessed be Yahweh who supports us.
Blessed be our God who encourages us.
Praise be to the Holy One who carries us
    day by day through all eternity.

Yahweh is the God who saves us.
Our God is a God who restores us
    and redeems us.
Yahweh is the One who rescues us
    from all that is evil.
The gracious One invites us
    into abundant life.

When we implore the destruction
    of those who injure us,
        when we plead with God to annihilate
        those who hurt our loved ones,
        when we ask the ruin
        of those who destroy our world,
Yahweh says: I hear your pain
    and I know your sorrow.
Yet even these I love
    and I desire to bring them back to me.

Though they flee to the farthest corners of the earth,
　though they hide in the depths of the ocean,
　they shall one day return to me,
　for I am God.

Who are you to deny my judgment?
Who are you to demand my vengeance?
Who are you to despise my mercy,
　a mercy that I pour out on all flesh?

Holy One, your wonderful design
　will finally be seen by all.
Your marvelous generosity
　will overcome all resistance.
Your loving embrace
　enfolds all peoples.
You tenderly hold
　the great and small.
You warmly encompass
　the old and young.
You kindly include
　the acceptable and outcast.
You ecstatically hug
　both saint and sinner.
No one is left out.

O God, let singers voice their joy
　before you.
Let musicians play
　their gladsome melodies.
Let young men and women
　dance their praise.
　while older folks raise their hands
　in reverent acclamation.

Praise our God, all you peoples.
May all you who love Yahweh
　raise a great paean of praise to God.

Join the mighty procession
of joyful songs.
From first to last and greatest to least,
sing the wonder of God.

Gracious One, turn us away
from violence.
Help us to embrace
the truth of your love.
Transform our avarice into generosity.
Turn us from selfish pursuits.
Grant us true knowledge of you
and fidelity to your cause.
Do not let us put inordinate value
on things of this world.
Bring us to an abiding trust in you.

Sing to Yahweh, all you peoples.
Raise your hands in Yahweh's praise.
Give thanks to the Alpha and Omega.
Listen to the One-Who-Is, life and light.
Proclaim God's fierce
and forever goodness.
Recount the awesome wonder
of our God's never-failing care.

Holy One, you give wisdom
to the people who desire you.
You give encouragement and hope
to those who seek you.
You give healing to the injured
and consolation to the desperate.
Praise Yahweh forever! Amen and amen.

69

Save me, O God, for I am sinking!
The waters of despair
    creep higher and higher.
I flail desperately
    and am close to drowning.
I am sliding, O God,
    sliding ever deeper
    into a swamp of hopelessness.
Whatever I grab to pull myself to safety
    breaks or crumbles
    or slips out of my hands.

I cry out to you for aid
    until I am weary.
My voice is garbled and cracked.
My eyes grow dim from weeping.
I look to you for rescue
    and you do not answer me.
Doubts swirl and dance
    like dust devils in my thoughts.
I am beseiged by fears.
My suspicions are countless.
Fears overtake me
    and dread chokes me.
I feel as if pitiless hands
    are around my neck,
    strangling the life from me.

Holy One, you know my sins.
You are aware of my stupidities.
You behold my limitations
    and see my weaknesses.
You perceive all the foolish things
    that I have done.
None of them are hidden from you.

The guilt of my sins and faults
　　are my daily bread.
The disgrace of my frailties
　　are my daily drink.
O keep me from hurting your people
　　because of my follies.
Keep me from harming
　　the creatures of this world
　　because of my failures and offenses.

You are my God and my all.
I search for you with open hands
　　and contrite heart.
I long for you with all my heart.

Great God, people insult me
　　because of my compassion.
I have become a laughingstock
　　because of my commitment to you.
I am made a stranger to my friends
　　because I defend your commands.
I am as a foreigner
　　and an alien to my family.

I fast and people make fun of my fasting.
I pray and people laugh at my praying.
They talk about me behind my back.
My efforts to follow you are ridiculed.
Gracious One, could it be
　　that I have taken my ideas
　　and made them yours?

Great God, I am angry
　　and want to strike back.
I yearn for the silencing
　　of those who ridicule me.
I long for the destruction
　　of those who slight you.

Strike them, Yahweh,
   as they strike at me!
Lift me from this anguish.
Lift me, O God, and save me!

Still, Holy One, I will turn to you.
I will trust you to answer me
   in your own time
   and in your own way.
You will answer me
   because of your great love.
You will rescue me
   because you are faithful
   to your promises.

You will keep me from sinking.
You will save me from drowning.
Don't let me fall into hopelessness.
Pull me from this swamp
   of doubt and fear.
Answer me, Holy One,
   because of your enduring love!
Out of your infinite compassion,
   come to me!
Do not hide yourself,
   for I am your servant.
Make haste to help me
   for I am in great distress.
Come and rescue me
   from this anguish!

You know how I am laughed at.
Insults have broken my heart
   and I am close to despair.
I looked for understanding
   and received the gall of hypocrisy.
I desired compassion
   and was given the vinegar of animosity.

Great God, could it be
   that I think only of myself
   and not of you, at all?

Holy One, I want to praise you
   with songs of joy.
I want to proclaim your greatness
   and give you thanks.
What will please you
   more than many sacrifices?
What do you desire more than
   much fasting and numerous prayers?

Doing justice with mercy
   are the sacrifices that please you.
Promoting peace among peoples
   are the works you desire.
Let those who are oppressed
   see and be glad.
Let all who seek you
   in dark and lonely places
   be encouraged.

Yahweh is close to the needy
   and the brokenhearted.
God does not forget the anguished
   and the oppressed.
O God, you will
   free your little ones from injustice
   and restore them
   with the gift of a radient new life.

Gracious One, let all creation praise you.
Let all living creatures praise you,
   for you give hope to the hopeless
   and give respect to the downtrodden.
You care for the destitute
   and rescue the desperate.

Great God, you are life and joy
   for all who love you.
Everyone is secure in your embrace.
Each one is totally fulfilled by you.
No one shall be taken from your hand.

70

Great God, I am back in the depths.
Misery and confusion assail me.
Doubt is my constant companion.
Holy One, I am afraid. Help me!

I am beset and overwhelmed.
I worry about becoming a laughingstock.
I don't want to be called a fool.
I am afraid of failing.
I am anxious about so many things.
I get angry when others sneer at me.
When my plans go awry,
   aggravation attacks me.
My thoughts are a tangled skein
   and my feelings are a jumble.

Great God, help me!
I have such a limited mind.
My understanding is so narrow.
I can be so foolish and stubborn.
Help me to seek you.
Help me to follow your path.

Holy One, help us all!
We are in such need.
May all who seek you be glad in you.
May they overflow with profound joy.

May everyone be grateful
   for your blessings.
And may each come to love you
   because of your steadfast care.
May we all say to you:
How great you are!
How good are your ways!

But I am so worn down
   and in such great need.
Come quickly to my aid!
You are my help and my savior.
Great God, do not delay!

71

The days and years slide quickly by.
Weeks and months flow swiftly away.
They are like water running through a sieve.
I am old now and my hair is gray.

Gracious One, I take refuge in you.
Great God, I turn to you.
You are my strength and my courage.
You have supported me from my youth.
You have protected me from my birth.
You have been with me faithfully
   from the moment I was conceived.
Thus I trust you and rely on you.
I will always give you thanks.
You are my hope and my joy.

My life is an example to many.
I praise you all the day.
At night I proclaim your goodness.

So do not leave me in my twilight years.
Do not forsake me now,
    when the feebleness of age is upon me.
Troubles still stalk me
    and weaknesses cause me to stumble.
I fear you will abandon me.

There are some who watch
    to take advantage of my infirmity.
They consult with each other
    to seize what they desire.
They act as if I am already dead.
They imagine there is no one to help me.

My God, be not far from me!
Great God, make haste to help me!

72

O God, this planet desperately needs
    your aid.
Our world utters piercing cries
    for help.
All the nations urgently need your assistance.

Holy One, raise up leaders for us,
    leaders who are filled with your Spirit,
    leaders who follow your ways.
May they be people
    of vision and courage
    who are imbued with your compassion.
May they be people
    who do justice for the poor
    and bring liberation to the oppressed.

May their deeds be like gentle rain
   encouraging new growth
   from a parched earth.

May their actions be like the spring sun
   which brings forth fresh life
   from newly warmed soil.
May they bring peace
   to the farthest reaches
   of our troubled planet.
O God, raise up for us leaders
   after your own heart.

Gracious One, raise up for us prophets
   who boldly speak your truth.
Raise up for us prophets
   who call us to you.
May they be filled with your wisdom
   and overflow with your mercy.
May they be like rivers of living water
   bringing refreshment to desolate lands.

May they give knowledge to the ignorant
   and new insight to the wisdom seeker.
May they inspire repentance
   and bring abundant life to those
   who sit in the shadow of death.
O God, raise up for us prophets
   who fearlessly speak your truth.

Faithful One, raise up for us workers
   who answer your call.
Raise up for us workers
   who reach out to the needy
   and aid the poor.
Raise up for us many, many workers
   who are rich in your goodness.

May they save the lives
  of the vulnerable
  and rescue the poor from destitution.
May they promote justice for all people.
May they abolish tyranny
  and purge every act of violence
  from our midst.
O God, raise up for us workers
  who answer your call.

Marvelous One, raise up for us singers
  who lift us in song.
Raise up for us singers
  who give glory to you.
May their melodies raise our hearts
  in a spirit of praise.
May their songs voice our gratitude
  for your goodness and love.
May they bring us laughter
  and dry our tears.
May they fill us with joy
  and heal the wounds of our souls.
O God, raise up for us singers
  who lift us in song.

Mysterious One, raise up for us weavers
  who weave us to one.
Raise up for us weavers
  who connect us in faith.
May they bring everyone
  from isolation into community
  and from alienation into belonging.
May they transform anarchy into order.
May they create meaning
  from the tangled threads of our lives
  and put purpose
  into the patterns of our days.

O God, raise up for us weavers
   who weave us to one.

Merciful One, raise up for us
   children who follow your way.
Raise up for us children
   who inspire us to play.
Raise up for us children
   who teach us to pray.
May our children be all that we hope for
   and all that they can be.
May they be graced in their lives
   and filled with your peace.
O God, raise up for us children
   who follow your way.

Praise Yahweh, all you peoples!
Because God alone
   does these wonderful things.
Praise our generous God.
May the glory of Yahweh
   shine forth from all the earth.
O God, may all generations praise you.

73

Holy One, here I am, full of conflict.
Once more I am inundated with anger.
Your word promises your favor
   for those who love you.

You promise your everlasting presence
   to the pure of heart.
But I am not one of these.

My faith is weak
  and jealousy plagues me.
I looked at those
  whose lives are filled with sin
  and envied their prosperity.
They seemed to have no pain.
They were healthy and strong.
They do not seem to endure
  the troubles of your followers.
They do not seem to suffer like me.

They wear pride like a badge of honor.
Violence envelops them
  like a heavy winter coat.
Like weeds, evil thoughts
  sprout in their minds   .
Their hearts are busy
  with malicious plots.
These laugh at the pious
  and despise the poor.
They boast about their deceitful plans.

Holy One, they frequently
  speak evil of you.
They arrogantly ascribe virtue
  to themselves
  while they seek to vanquish goodness
  with their schemes.
And people say nothing against them.
Neighbors find no fault with them.

These schemers are always at ease.
They get richer and richer
  while I am afflicted morning to night.
I wonder: Have I followed your way
  in vain?
Is my hope and trust in you utter folly?

Then, great God, I cry aloud to you:
Do you not know my troubles?
Do you not see the prosperity
  of those who laugh at you?
Why is this the way it is?

I tried to understand and was baffled.
Then, Holy One, you helped me grasp
  the reality of their lives.
You let me see the terror
  which haunts the arrogant
  and stalks the tyrannical.
You showed me
  the horror that pursues the wicked
  at every moment of their lives.
Though these people will utterly deny it,
  each feels total dread
  which they try to conceal.
Each tries to hide their fears,
  even from themselves.
But, Holy One, they can not hide
  their intense anxiety from you.

They worry about being swept away.
They are tormented by thoughts
  that they will disappear and be gone
  as in the twinkling of an eye.
They fear to have their lives
  fall into total ruin.
They are alarmed by the belief
  that they will lose everything in death.
They panic at the thought
  of the end of their lives.
They assume that when they die
  they will have nothing
  and they believe
  no one will mourn their passing.
They go alone into the dark.

Already, in their heart of hearts,
   they see themselves to be phantoms.
They perceive themselves to be ghosts
   who are of no value, even to themselves.

Such anxieties pierce them
   in the night
   and prick them with stray thoughts
   throughout the day.
They seek to forget.
But they cannot quite
   drown out the noise of these fears
   with wine and riotous living.

Therefore I indeed understood
   that my bitter thoughts were stupid.
My envious feelings were foolish.
My pride was wounded by my folly.
But I now have peace
   in the depths of my heart.

Gracious One, I do not understand you.
But I desire always to be near you.
Hold me close and guide me
   with your Spirit.
Teach me and I will have life.

Great God, you are the Center
   of my being.
You are all that I desire.
Your loving providence
   surrounds me.
You are my strength
   even when my body fails.
You are my courage
   when my spirit withers.
You are my heart
   and inheritance forever.

Draw even those who have forgotten you
   from the destruction they so eagerly pursue.
Bring all who are far from you
   into the shelter of your loving heart.
Let all peoples see how wonderful you are.
Let them truly understand
   how great it is to be near you.
Then all of us will be secure,
   secure in your tender embrace forever.

74

Great God, is nothing sacred anymore?
Are integrity and faithfulness forgotten?
Can everything be purchased for a price?
Is there nothing reliable
   to which I can cling?

O God, your will is proclaimed
   by those who think they know you
   and yet they are far from you.

They twist your word
   to suit themselves
   and do not recognize
   their own distortions.
They create you in their own image
   and do not notice what they have done.
Then we foolishly follow their lead.

Holy One, is nothing honored anymore?
Those who are honest are scorned.
They who are faithful are mocked.
Great God, we make ourselves into gods.

People run panting
   after their own cravings.
The effect of their actions
   is not considered.
The value of their desires
   for the good of the community
   is not important.

The poor are dispensable.
The vulnerable are swept away.
The earth, the air, and the many waters
   are not valued anymore.
These are raped and polluted
   by an insatiable lust for wealth.

Animals and plants,
   together with cultures and human persons,
   are carelessly, violently destroyed.
Pain and suffering stalks the land.
Sickness and violent death abounds.
Is nothing truly valued anymore?

Yahweh, where are you?
Where are the people
   who will speak your truth
   and lead us to life?
The people who profess religion
   do not live it.
Those who declare they know you
   are as corrupt and false
   as the people who deny you.

Holy One, why do you allow it?
How can you bear it?
Where is hope?
Where is your rescuing
   and renewing power
   in this crass and careless world?

Yet you are the Creator
   of the universe.
You hold all things in being.
This crazy, hurting world
   depends on you.
This planet is kept firm
   by your sustaining will.
Without you, nothing can exist.

Remember your covenant, O God.
Remember your promises
   from of old.
Remember your people
   whom you love
   with an unquenchable love.

Again raise up for us prophets
   as of old.
Lift up for us teachers
   of your word.
Bring forth for us leaders
   after your own heart.
Create for us people of integrity
   who do your will.

Holy One, where violence abounds
   let peace multiply.
Where sickness is epidemic
   let health blossom forth.
Where people starve
   provide a surplus of food.
Where the world is abused
   let new care arise.
And where the poor are oppressed
   let justice prevail.
Where the needy are put to shame
   let respect be the rule.

Come, great and gracious Mystery!
Come and restore the earth!
Come and renew our world!
Come and reclaim our hearts!
Help us, O God, and let all the peoples
   see your glory.

75

O glorious One, how merciful you are.
How great is your goodness.
You are, indeed, our saving God.
We praise you with all our hearts.
We thank you for you are with us.
The peoples sing joyfully
   of your wondrous deeds.
You care for all people
   and renew the earth.
You are our saving God.

Generous One, you say to us:
I have set my time for judgment
   and I will judge with equity.
Though the earth quakes
   and every creature trembles,
I will keep the foundations firm.
Nothing is lost from my hand.
I am your saving God.

O peoples, do you not see?
Ultimate judgment comes from God.
It does not come from people or angels.
O nations, do you not know?
God's final word is not found
   in any social order or in history itself.

True judgment is yours, great God.
You are our saving God.

Every living thing must come to you.
Every person will come
    before you at last:
    the strong and the weak,
    the arrogant and the humble,
    the rich and the poor.
Everyone will see your love.
You are our saving God.

Then you will show for all to see,
    authentic courage and genuine cowardice.
You will make manifest to all
    true riches and real poverty.
You will reveal unmitigated arrogance
    and authentic humility.

Each will perceive
    the depths of their failures
    and acclaim the transforming power
    of your love.
You are our saving God.

All will understand your offer of mercy
    in the fire of your unbounded truth.
Each will be free to choose life with you
    or death in separation from you.
Those who choose life will rejoice
    eternally with you.
You are our saving God.

I will never stop speaking of you, my God.
I will never stop declaring your goodness
    nor will I cease proclaiming your love.
Suffering shall be no more
    and evils will end.

While those who love you
    are filled with everlasting joy.

Blessed be Yahweh, always and everywhere.
Blessed be our saving God, now and forever.

76

Gracious and Holy One,
    we are joyful in prosperous days
    and mournful in times of sorrow.
But in both joy and sorrow
    you are near to us.

In days of peace and plenty
    we praise you.
Amid times of trouble and grief we thank you,
    for you are our comfort and our strength.

Thank you, merciful One,
    for you let yourself be known by us.
Your glory shines among your people.
Your presence is established on the earth.
Your dwelling place
    is in the midst of this world.
Peace is your garment
    and justice your cloak.
Weapons are broken
    and war is no more.

You are glorious, most loving One.
You hover like a mother over her children.
You are like an ever vigilant father
    who safeguards his family.

You are marvelous, most faithful One.
You are from everlasting to everlasting
    in your steadfast concern for our good.

Those who rebel gain no glory.
Those who turn away procure no security.
Strength and craftiness are useless before you.
Threats and plots turn into nothingness.
The powerful are rebuked by your word.
The malicious are thwarted by your designs.

O God, how awesome you are.
Who can stand in your presence?
Your judgments are true.
They manifest absolute justice.
All your verdicts
    harmonize justice with mercy
    in a perfect symmetry.
Nothing confutes your wisdom.
The earth stands in silent wonder.
All the oppressed of every nation
    are released in joy.

All humankind will praise you.
Your goodness will be proclaimed
    over all the earth.
Your steadfast care will be shouted
    from the housetops.
Your blessed little ones will rejoice.

O peoples, keep the promises
    you make to Yahweh.
Bring your gifts of faithful service
    to our gracious and merciful God.
Reverence the Holy One
    and keep God's commands,
    for Yahweh humiliates the proud
    but raises the humble from the dust.

77

Because I am desolate, O God,
I cry out to you.
Desperately, I seek you.
Day and night I look for you.
Night and day I stretch out my hands
    to you in prayer.

Yet I find no consolation.
Again and again, I sigh and think of you.
I faithfully meditate on your word.
Yet my heart remains dry as dust.
My spirit faints within me.

I can not sleep at night.
Anxiety overwhelms me.
Once more I groan:
Holy One, where are you?
Have you abandoned me?
Have you ceased to love me?
Have you forsaken your promises
    and forgotten your mercy?
Has your compassion
    turned to indifference?

Then, great God, I think: I am lost!
I fear you have gone away.
I am grief stricken
    because you are silent.
But then I remember
    your glorious deeds
    and recall the wonders
    you did in past times.
I remember you are Who-You-Are.
There is none like you.

Yet again, Holy One, I think
   of your graciousness.
I meditate on all you have done.
Your way, O God, is holy.
There is no God but you.

You are the One
   who does miracles.
You showed your love
   amid your people
   and displayed your care
   among the nations.
You rescue your people
   and redeem the world.

The great forces of nature obey you.
You tame the whirlwind
   and calm the raging sea.
You turn away the lightning
   and change a thunderous downpour
   into a gentle rain.
The wondrous beauties of this planet
   are your fingerprints.
Its rich diversity of life
   are your footprints.

Holy One, you rescue
   and renew your people.
Rescue me, my God; I wait for you.

78

Listen to me, O people of the earth!
Hear what I want to say!

I will tell you the stories of our past.
I will speak the sagas which were told to me.
I will relate the tales of our ancestors.
I will recount these epics for the children.
They will hear of the great deeds
    of our God.
They will know of the wonders
    that Yahweh has done.

Long ago Yahweh created the universe.
God filled the cosmos with galaxies of stars
    and eventually formed this little planet
    from the stuff of stars.
The earth cooled and life emerged
    through Yahweh's creative power.
Eons passed and life forms multiplied
    through Yahweh's resourceful imagination.

And from this wondrous mix
    of living beings,
Yahweh brought forth
    a self-reflective entity
    called 'homo sapiens.'
    and began a journey with them.
The way was dark and long.
Humans did not understand their Creator.
People created gods for themselves
    and they were afraid.

It appears, from the beginning
    fear reigned.
People turned against people.
And nation rose against nation.
Nothing and no one was secure.
It seems, since the beginning,
    war has begotten war
    and violence has multiplied violence
    of every kind.

People were lost,
   not knowing God's way.
Still Yahweh embraced them
   with love
   and tried to teach them the path
   of generosity and compassion.
Yahweh's way leads to justice
   and peace for all peoples.

But the peoples turned away.
They refused to listen to a God
   who asked generosity and compassion.
They rejected a God who asked justice
   for all life forms.

Many times Yahweh sought
   to gather the peoples
   and many times they turned away.
Yet Yahweh continued to work
   and to bless every generation.

The gracious One provides ways
   and creates means for peoples
   to have abundant life.
God gives rest to the weary
   and strength to the burdened.
Yahweh brings healing to the sick
   and comfort to the afflicted.
Still people turn away.

The Holy One made the sun and moon
   to provide light when it was dark.
The gracious One made fire
   to give warmth when it was cold.
Yahweh supplied water to drink
   and food to eat.
Still people turned away.

Humans are the only creatures
   who kill each other in anger
   and maim each other from malice.
People are the only species
   who wantonly destroy
   each other and this world.

Envy provokes murder.
Sloth incites slavery.
Greed enkindles insatiable cravings.
Lust foments endless entanglements.
Pride ignites anger
   and a contumacious spirit.
War and disease quickly ensue.
Torture and death soon follow.
Entire peoples are slaughtered.
Whole species disappear.
Nothing is safe and nothing is sacred.

Political leaders urge the destruction
   of perceived traitors
   in the name of honor and national security.
Religious leaders exhort
   the destruction of perceived heretics
   to protect their concept of truth.
All avidly pursue their own advantage
   and oppression rules with an iron fist.

History overflows with violence.
Violence becomes multitudinous
   rushing rivers of pain.
This pain, in turn,
   creates oceans of sorrow.
The people cry out for pity and relief.
And, O God, you did have pity.

Again and again you inspired people
   to speak out against oppression.

But, again and again, these were silenced.
Over and over, they were destroyed
   by the fearful and powerful of this world.

Some whom you called
   feared reprisal and refused to act.
Others whom you called
   lacked sufficient trust in your goodness
   and turned away.
Still, you found a few
   to urge justice and seek for peace.
But yet again, the fearful and powerful refused to hear.

So you reached out again.
You called a man and a woman
   to create a people for yourself.
They agreed to be your people
   and you agreed to be their God.
You led them in your ways
   and taught them your laws.

You commanded them
   to teach their children,
   to tell them of your law and love,
   so succeeding generations
   would trust you and set their hope in you.
But these children, too,
   soon turned away
   to pursue their own desires.

Yet you continued to protect this people
   and kept them from total destruction.
You continued to lead and aid them.
With mighty deeds you freed this people
   from bondage and guided them
   through deserts of folly.
You led them and fed them
   through barren lands of resistance.

You were with them through years
  of stubbornness and stupidity.

Again and again, you helped them
  and showed them the way
  out of slavery and into freedom.
You led them toward abundant life.
Still, each generation continued to rebel.

Though overwhelmed many times
  by violence and disaster,
  you preserved a few
  of this chosen people.
And from that remnant
  you brought forth
  a faithful and beloved Child,
  in whom you fully dwelt.

This Child would call all peoples
  to your way of justice and peace,
  and show this world your path
  of generosity and compassion.

Your beloved Child
  was murdered too,
  nailed to a cross
  by the fearful and powerful.
But you raised up your
  beloved and faithful One,
  to Fullness of Life with you.
You promised your Spirit
  and this new life
  to all who followed him.

Your little ones saw and rejoiced.
The people who believed were glad.
A new kind of life
  was made available to all.

Whoever will accept this gift of new life,
  whoever will seek to live your path
  of justice and peace,
  will know your fullness and life.

But fear still stalks the land.
Violence and greed wreak havoc
  on the earth.
Human beings still rend and kill
  each other.
Stupidity and ignorance,
  avarice and envy,
  still turn this world into a desert
  and hearts to stone.

Words are twisted
  to support the status quo.
Ideas familiar to the fearful
  are the only ones accepted.
Systems that advantage the powerful
  are the only ones tolerated.
So the poor and despised
  continue to cry out for mercy
  as their stomachs cry out for bread.

But still, we tell the story from of old:
  how you, gracious One, liberate and feed;
  how you, Yahweh, heal and teach;
  how you bring people into New Life;
  how you bless the little ones of this earth;
  and how you, Holy One, create living hearts
  from hearts of stone.

O God, a deep peace of soul
  is your gift to your people.
Security of spirit is the heritage
  of those who follow you.
You are with your people in compassion.

You are with this world in truth.
You give new life, your eternal life,
    to those who seek to follow your way.

The fearful and powerful may rage.
They may bring destruction upon the earth.
But you are there, Holy One,
    to save your faithful little ones.
And you continue to inspire people
    to proclaim your truth
    and live your way of love.

How great you are, Holy One!
How deep your compassion!
How fulfilling your ways!
You are the leaven that will lift
    the whole world.
You are the light that enlightens our souls.
You are the justice that will lead us to peace.
You are the new wine that will shatter
    the old wineskins of violence and fear.

O God, your wisdom and love will prevail.
You are both life and love.
You are the living power
    who will reclaim all humankind.
Praise Yahweh forever.

79

Holy God, evil bestrides the land.
Injustice is epidemic in our world
    and your servants suffer.

Your little ones are despised.
Your people are exploited
  and your prophets are murdered.
This is not just! It is not right!

The people who prosper are those
  who do not reverence you.
They scorn your commands
  and grind your little ones into the dust.

My heart cries out to you, O God.
My spirit says: Repay them!
Repay them seven times seven
for each of their crimes.
Repay them seven times seven
  for all their insults.
Great God, I desire their destruction
  because they have destroyed your people.
Devastate them, as they have devastated
  the works of your hands.
Then your people will rejoice.
They will shout aloud with thanksgiving.

But, Holy One, you reply: Patience!
You say to me: Peace!
You say to me:
I will answer your pain.
I recognize but will not answer
  your anger,
    because violence begets violence.

O God, you say to me:
I-Am-Who-I-Am.
Nothing good is ever lost
  from my hand.
All things are held in my plan.
Patience! Peace!
Love! Trust!

And one day you will rejoice with me.
For you will see the work
   that I accomplish
   even among sinners
   and those who go astray.

I hear you, my beloved, my little ones!
Let my patience be in you
   and peace fill you.
Let my love enfold you.
All things are in my hand!

80

O shepherd of your people, hear us!
O you who lead your flock,
   have mercy on us!
You who sustain the universe, help us!
Come and rescue us!
Restore us, O God,
   and by the gift of your Spirit,
   make us whole and new.

Great God, we feel lost and afraid.
We call out to you and you are silent.
We eat the bread of many sorrows.
We drink from the cup of many troubles.
We are laughed at and scorned.
Restore us, O God,
   and by the wisdom of your Spirit,
   make us whole and new.
So often in the past you protected us.
You kept us secure.

You created us in love,
　　and faithfully watched over us.
You even sent us Jesus, your Beloved One,
　　to show us the way to freedom,
　　to lead us out of the slavery of sin,
　　and to heal our afflictions.
Restore us, O God,
　　and by your gentle Spirit
　　make us whole and new.

When we strayed
　　you brought us back to you.
You led us to pleasant places
　　and pastured us in green meadows.
You planted us as your cherished garden
　　and nurtured us as loving gardeners
　　tend their favorite plants.

But now we are in dire distress.
Our hopes are trampled.
Our dreams are shattered.
Our visions of peace and plenty are destroyed.

Great God, our land is overrun.
It is trampled by wild animals.
Our pleasant pastures are a wasteland.
We are threatened on every side.

Restore us, O God,
　　and by the glorious power of your Spirit
　　make us whole and new.
Preserve and protect your people,
　　your little ones whom you love.
Keep us faithful to you
　　and we will always praise you.
Restore us, O God,
　　and show us your mercy.
Then we are made whole and new.

81

Sing joyfully to Yahweh
  who is our strength.
Shout your gladness to God
  who provides for all our needs.

Raise your voice in thanksgiving
  to the Holy One who rescues us.
Proclaim your gratitude
  with hymns of praise
  to this gracious Mystery
  who rescues and renews us.

Make music with pipes and harps.
Give thanks with trumpets and cymbals.
Shout praise with drums and dancing,
  for Yahweh, our God, has saved us.

Holy One, we celebrate your goodness.
Gracious One, we rejoice in your mercy.
Loving One, we remember your gift to us
  in the Child of your heart, Jesus the Christ.

He is the gift of your saving power,
  a saving power shown to us
  in his passing over,
  through death to new life with you.

Jesus is your Beloved and our brother.
He is the gift of your saving power,
  given to us when we pass through death,
  through death to new life with you

We rejoice in this great gift to us.
We celebrate this great work for us.
We recognize the gift of your Spirit to us.

And we joyfully proclaim the gift
   of your Spirit-With-Us,
      each day of our lives.

Your Spirit dwells with us
   in the depths of our hearts.
Your Spirit works in us
   in the most secret parts of our souls.
Your Spirit is a revealing light.
It is your penetrating voice.
It is your compassionate smile.

Your Spirit comes with knowledge
   and says to us:
I lift the burden of fear from you.
I free you from the chains of sorrow.
I release you from guilt for your sins.
When you call to me in distress
I will answer you and heal you.
I touch the very core of your being.
Fear not! Come and rest in my love.

Hear me, O my people, while I teach you.
Listen to me, O my beloved little ones.
Keep my ways of service and compassion.
Speak the truth and do no wrong.
Make no god of things or people
   or any created good.

Let nothing stand between us
   for I am Yahweh, your God.
It is I who rescue and redeem you.
Let me feed you with my word.
Let me fill you with my gladness.
Open your mind to receive my Spirit.
Open your heart
   and I will freely dwell with you.

There are many who will not listen to my voice.
There are many more who are afraid of me.
Others are ashamed to come to me
    and some refuse me out of stubborn pride.

Still, I pursue every one of these.
I am the hound of heaven
    ever present to their inmost being.
Though they know it not,
I surround each of them with love.

O my people, listen
    while I teach you.
O my beloved little ones,
    follow my ways of service
    and compassion toward all.

I will come quickly when you are in distress.
I will turn your sorrow into joy.
I will feed you with the finest wheat.
I will quench your thirst
    with living waters.

Joy will be yours, poured out in plenty,
    sweet as honey from the comb.
You will be totally satisfied
I will quench your thirst forever.

82

Yahweh, you are the source of all life.
You uphold everything in being.
You are the final destiny of all that exists.
Like a mother hen hovers over her chicks,
    you brood over your creation.

You search for justice among all peoples.
You seek for equity among the nations.

Your Spirit speaks to us saying:
Do justice in all your works
    and do not be partial in your judgments.
Your Spirit declares:
    do not take advantage of another's troubles
    and defend those who have no power.

Your Spirit proclaims:
    Be an advocate for the needy
    and a friend to the helpless.
Your Spirit urges:
    Do what you can to free people
    from every form of oppression.
Do not let justice disappear
    from the earth.

Holy One, you declare to us:
    my precious little ones,
    you are my beloved.
I am with you always.

All people are my beloved children.
May they walk in my ways!
Though your great ones seek
    to make themselves gods
    and your strong ones believe
    they are invincible,
    these too shall die.
They shall pass away
    and this planet shall see them no more.
Every person and every thing
    in the universe comes to its appointed end.

Come Yahweh, and renew the earth
All the nations belong to you.

83

Gracious One, we are sorely wounded.
We are harried and beleaguered.
It seems that all the destroying powers
   of this world seek our extermination.
They plot our downfall
   and desire our demise.
Fear is our daily bread.
Our cup of harassment overflows.

Great God, we look to you,
   who are our help.
We turn to you who are our only hope.
We are surrounded and brought very low.
We are falling into the grave.

O God, have you forgotten us?
Where are you in this travail?
We look to you who are our help.
We turn to you who are our only hope.

Come to us! Holy One.
You are our fortress and shield.
Come, now, to our aid!
For you are our light and our joy.
Change these plots into ashes.
Turn these schemes to naught.
We look to you who are our help.
We turn to you who are our only hope.

Come, O God, our rock and redeemer!
Come to us, our strength and our shield!
We remember your promises of old.
We remember your saving power.
We remember the great works
   you have done for us.

We turn to you who are our help.
We turn to you who are our only hope.
We shall not be overcome.
We shall bless you forever.

84

O God, how lovely it is to dwell with you.
From the depths of my spirit
I long for your presence.
My whole being yearns for you, my God.
I ache for you like a weary wanderer
    aches for home.

O gracious One, you are my Beloved.
You are my God and my All.
When I am filled by your nearness
    my heart is inundated with joy.
My mind and body overflow with delight.

All creatures find a home with you.
Each is held in your loving embrace.
Happy the people who feel your love.
Joyful are they who recognize your care.
They are always singing your praises
    with great joy and thanksgiving.

Happy are all who trust in you.
You are their courage and strength.
They know your presence
    in their inmost being.

You make the rough places smooth
    and the dry places to flow
    with living water.

Those who follow you
  grow in love and mercy
  as they travel life's path.
They know you
  in all the moments of their lives.

My God, one day in your presence
  is more wonderful
  than a billion times a billion days
  spent elsewhere.

I would rather be the least of your servants
  than the most exalted of this world's rulers.
For you are my guardian and my guide.
You are the very heart of my soul.
You are my only delight.

You bless your people
  with immense kindness.
You respect and honor your little ones.
You provide good things
  for all whom you love.

You are the source of every happiness
  and center of all good.
You are a deep well of repose
  in every circumstance.

O gracious One, hear me!
O Holy One, listen to my plea.
Bless your people,
  the people you have chosen.

Yes, great God, how happy are all
  who trust in you!

85

Glorious and gracious One,
   you have given us so much.
You prospered our nation.
You forgave our sins.
You provided health and strength.
You bestowed times of peace
   and seasons of happiness.

You endowed us with beautiful things.
You put many good people
   in our lives
   and poured out a flood
   of wonderful experiences.

But now we are hurting.
Our land is troubled and sin abounds.
So many chase after other gods.
Multitudes seek only fame and fortune.
Others pursue a painless existence
   in the oblivion of drugs or alcohol.
Some have fallen into apathy
   and others wallow in despair.
Still more bask in angry bitterness.
Many run in fear from you,
   as from a vengeful ogre.
They fear your wrath.
They fear you will obliterate them
   because of their sins and weaknesses.

O God, help us to listen to you.
Help us to understand
   and accept
   your unchanging word to us.
Your promise to us is peace
Your pledge to us is forgiveness.

And your assurance to us
   is release and new life,
   if we but turn to you with contrite heart.

Your word is true when we turn to you.
Love and faithfulness rush out to greet us.
Justice and peace joyfully seek
   to embrace us.
You choose each of us
   and desire to carry all of us back to you.

Thus our society will prosper
   and we shall again see your glory.
In the land of the living
   we shall once more
know your presence,
   and faithfulness will flourish.
Right relationships will be established.
No one will go hungry.
Sorrow will be turned to joy.

All will feast at the table of justice.
Righteousness will pour forth
   to create a place of honor for us
   among all the nations of the earth.

86

Great God, hear my cry
   and answer me!
   for I am alone and helpless.
Save me from disaster
For I am your devoted servant.
I trust in You-Who-Are.
You are my God and my All.

Bring joy back to my spirit.
My heart searches for you
My soul reaches out to you.
Hear me and help me
    for I cry to you all the day.
Listen to me in my trouble
    because I need you!
Most humbly I implore you:
Answer me!

Gracious One, you are good
    and forgiving.
Your steadfast love
    is an ever-flowing spring.
You are a torrent of mercy
    poured out on all who turn to you.

Holy One, nothing is like you.
Your works are so glorious.
They reach far ahead of
    our most marvelous hopes.
They proceed farther than
    our greatest dreams.
You are the Alpha and Omega.
    And you do wonderful things.
You alone are God.

All the nations shall come to you.
All the peoples will reverence you.
They will praise you
    for being Who-You-Are.
They will give you thanks
    for all your blessings.
They will worship you
    with eternal gratitude and joy.

Teach me your way, my God,
    that I may walk steadfastly in your truth.

Give me a faithful spirit,
    that I may reverence you
    with my whole being.
I will thank you with all my heart.
I will proclaim your goodness forever.

Holy One, how great
    is your enduring love!
How marvelous your goodness!
You delivered me
    from the depths of despair.
You have saved me from death itself.

Yet I am still beset and weak.
Thoughts cause me to stumble.
Feelings overwhelm me
    and events drag me down.
My daily journey is painfully difficult.
I have nowhere to turn but to you.

Great God, you are merciful
    and your care is ever gracious.
You are slow to anger
    and abounding in steadfast kindness.
You are faithful in all your works.
You keep your promises
    to every generation.
Turn to me and have mercy on me.
Give me strength and courage.
Grant me your wisdom
    and keep me obedient to your call.
Save me, because I love you.

Help me, my God,
    so that those who know me
    may see your goodness
    and give you thanks.

Let them see your kindness,
    so that they too will turn to you.
They will come to you
    because you helped me
    and comforted me.

87

Great and glorious God,
Jerusalem is a symbol
    of your covenant love
    and the earth is an image
    of your creative fruitfulness.
Holy One, the universe is an icon
    of your magnificent greatness.
Nothing escapes your loving embrace.

O God, happy are the people
    who listen to your word.
Happy are the people
    who remember the wonderful things
    you have done.

You love all of your creation,
    every particle of it,
    from the greatest to the least.
Every people, every tribe,
    and every nation
    is enfolded in your infinite care.

Those who love you know your presence.
Those who follow you
    know a joy in their hearts
    that nothing can take away.

Those who love you are counted
    as citizens of your kin-dom.
They participate in your eternal creativity.
They are a peaceable community
    sharing in your life forever.

O God, you are the Source and the Goal.
You are the repository of endless bliss.
Happy are all who turn to you.
Happy are all who call upon you.
They shall live with you eternally.

88

Yahweh, at night I cry out to you.
Come, rescue and liberate me!
I raise my hands to you in prayer
    for you are my only hope.

Holy One, hear me!
My heart is sorely burdened.
My spirit is mortally laden.
There is nothing before me
    but the emptiness of the grave.

My strength is gone
    and my courage has fled.
I am helpless and hopeless.
I feel as useless as a broken pot
    and as forgotten as last year's news.

Yahweh, I am in deepest despair.
I feel condemned and overwhelmed.

My friends shun me.
I am a laughingstock
  to those who know me.
I am a joke and a fool
  to the world.
I am lost and trapped
  in my own spinning thoughts.
My eyes grow dim with sorrow.
My spirit is paralyzed with grief.

Great God, once more
I call out to you.
Gracious One, again
I plead with you.
Hear my cry!
Listen to my anguish!
See my need!
Turn to me and rescue me.

Do you work wonders for the dead?
Do those in their graves praise you?
Do those who have died
  know your steadfast love?
Are miracles seen by those long gone?
Are you there with your saving power
in death as well as in life?

Great God, one more time
I cry out to you: Save me!
Where are you?
Have you rejected me?
Have you abandoned me?

From my childhood
I have struggled to be faithful.
From my youngest days
I have suffered much.
Death has always been close to me.

I am worn out.
I am crushed and destroyed.
All day long I am flooded with misery.
All night long anguish visits my bed.
I am closed in on every side.
I am abandoned by family and friends.
Only darkness companions me.

89

Merciful One, I will proclaim
  your steadfast love which is forever.
I will speak your faithfulness
  which flows out to all peoples.
I will declare your constant care
  which is from everlasting to everlasting.

Your fidelity is more constant
  than the speed of light.
Your love is more real
  than the existence of the universe.
Your care is more dependable
  than the rising and setting of the sun.

Holy One, you made a covenant
  with our ancestors for all generations.
You promised your enduring love.
You will always be with us.
You will never desert us.

All the earth proclaims your glory.
Your creation sings your faithfulness.
Nothing compares with you.
All existence comes from you.
Nothing exists without you.

Reverence is our fitting response.
Respectful joy and thanksgiving fill our hearts.
Things turn to dust and fame fades away.
Power evaporates to naught
   and beauty can perish.

The people who worship power
   and those who seek after material things
   will disappear like the morning mist.
The people who pursue fame
   and those who destroy beauty
   will vanish like dew in the morning sun.

O God, at your command
   raging seas are quieted.
By your sovereign will
   ruthless schemes collapse
   and cruel tyrannies dissolve.

The whole universe is enfolded
   in your loving embrace.
Earth and sea, sky and stars,
   are all carefully held close to your heart.

Each atom and molecule
   sings your creativity.
Every living creature
   joyfully proclaims your glory.

Your steadfast love is revealed
   in all you do.
Happy are they who recognize your kindness.
Happy are all who know your faithful care.
Because of you, these rejoice
   in every moment
   and praise your goodness all the day.
You wish for honest living
   from each person.

You want compassion
   given to all peoples.
You desire justice in every land
   and peace among the nations.

Your kin-dom is the way
   of compassion and service.
You, gracious One, are our guardian
   and our guide.
You are our All in all.
Blessed be You-Who-Are forever.

You speak to every person
   in their inmost heart.
You call us to be faithful
   to your way of trust and love.
You set the seal of your Spirit
   within each of us.
You name us your special friends
   and call us your beloved little ones.

As you chose the rulers of times past
   to serve you and be your faithful stewards,
   so you choose each of us
   so we may serve you
   and be your faithful stewards.

As you you chose the prophets of old,
   to be your friends and speak for you,
   so you choose all of us
   to be your friends
   and speak your way of loving service.

As you called Jesus, your Beloved,
   and showed us your heart through him,
   so you call every one of us
   to be your beloved companions
   and your presence in our hurting world.

Now we see.
It is a great mystery, but true.
You, indeed, call each of us
　　to be your stewards and your friends.
You choose every one of us
　　to speak your word
　　and declare your love.
You desire all of us to be close to you
　　as your beloved companions
　　and faithful little ones.

You will anoint us
　　with the oil of gladness
　　as you pour out your Holy Spirit
　　on all flesh.
Your Spirit shall be upon us
　　to strengthen and protect us.
All things do work for the good
　　of those who love you.

Your faithfulness will uphold us.
We can depend upon your steadfast love.
We can say: "Abba," "Amma,"
　　and "my Beloved" to you, great God
　　with joyful heart.
We can proclaim: "our God and our All"
　　in ecstatic adoration.

Holy One, you are the source of all good.
You renew and reclaim the earth.
From the greatest to the least,
　　you pour out everlasting joy
　　upon all persons.
All will be filled to overflowing
　　with abundant life in you.
You keep your promises.
Your covenant is forever.

Yahweh proclaims:
When people follow their own designs
   and refuse to follow my ways,
     they will suffer the awful consequences
     that are inherent in the very nature
     of their choices.

The Holy Mystery declares:
   When people violate my commandments
   and shun the commitment
   I set before them,
   they shall find
   that sorrow and disaster will plague them,
   while pain and loss will be their lot.

The great God says:
How my heart sorrows
   when people reject me and desert me.
How I am saddened
   when they turn their back to me.
How much I am anguished
   when anyone destroys
   the beauty of my creation.

Yet the One-Who-Is vows:
I will not remove my steadfast love.
Neither will I abandon my faithfulness.
I will not renounce my covenant
   nor change my decree.
Once, and for all eternity,
I have promised, by my holiness itself,
I will never stop loving you.

I will watch over you as a mother
   watches over her child.
The sun shall be my faithful witness.
The moon shall be a steadfast reminder
   of my promises to you.

Indeed, even if the sun should fail
    or the moon no longer shine,
    my pledges will never cease.
I will not be overcome.
Selfishness will be seen as foolish.
Cynicism will be regarded as futile.
Greed will be viewed as useless.
Pride shall be broken and discarded.
Panting after power will be rejected
    and coveting wealth shall be forsaken.
Lies and stealing will be condemned.
Anger and envy will be disgraced.

Praise our God forever!
Amen and amen.

90

Holy God, you are our home
    through all generations.
Before you created the universe
    or brought our world to be,
    you chose us to be with you.

With you there is no beginning and no end,
    for you are the One-Who-Is.
A thousand years are like a minute to you.
The minute is here and then it is gone.
A billion years are but an hour for you.

You are aware of every instant of time
    at the same moment of time.
So, for you there is no duration.
There is simply an eternal now.

But at the instant you planned for us
   in your eternal now,
   you called each of us into being.
And in the fullness of time
   you call each of us back to you.
We name this birth and death.

We are afraid of death.
This unknown overwhelms us.
Our days are shadowed by anxiety.
Our years are like a sigh.
Our lives are like a dream
   that fades as we awake.
We quickly grow, like a plant
   that sprouts in the morning,
   flowers at noon,
   and by evening light fades and dies.

Our days on earth are soon over.
We can hope for eighty good years
   or perhaps ninety, if we are strong.
Each day brings its problems
   as well as joys.
The time is soon gone.
We are seen no more.

Most gracious One, turn us to you
   and have compassion on us.
Teach us to rightly value our days
   that we may be wise.
Show us your steadfast love.
Help us to rejoice and be glad
   in your gift of life to us.

Let us live lives full of meaning
   and bless us with a lively purpose
   through all of our years.

May we know great happiness
   as well as the sorrows
   that come to us along the way.
And may your purposes
   be accomplished in everything we do.

91

You who dwell
   in the presence of Yahweh,
   who abide in the shadow of our God,
   say to the One-Who-Is-With-You:
You are the gracious One
   in whom I trust.

You keep me safe from dangers.
You deliver me from traps.
When I am near you
I am safe from harm.
Always be my protector
   and defend me from every peril.

Your faithfulness is solid.
You are like a giant rock
   standing amid the tides
   of an uncertain future.
I need not dread any dangers.
I will not fear troubles or woes.
Neither sickness nor injury
   nor a multitude of afflictions
   shall triumph over me.
Your love is the firm foundation
   upon which I safely stand.

My God, I trust you.
No matter what the threat,
I shall not be moved.
No matter what the situation,
I shall not be afraid.

I shall live to see
   the appearance of some good,
   even from terrible events.
Because, great God, you forever work
   to bring forth the good from each choice.
You forever work in every circumstance
   for the good of all your creation.

Your sustaining Spirit upholds me.
You keep this world from destruction.
You are with me all my days.
Fierce and cunning tongues
   shall not harm me.
These will crumble away into dust.

Great God, you continue to declare:
I am Who-I-Am
   and I watch over all that I love.
I rescue the people who call on me.

O people, call on me and I will answer.
I am with you and I bless you.
I give you of my life.
I give you of my very self
   and reveal to you my salvation.

92

How good it is and how glorious
    to sing your praise, great God.
How wonderful it is to give you thanks.
Each morning we declare
    your constant love.
    and thank you for your gracious goodness.
Each night we affirm your faithfulness
    and praise you for your tender mercy.

We sing our thanksgiving
    in the words and music of our songs.
We voice our gratitude
    in the melody of our lives.
Your infinite kindnesses make us glad.
We are filled with joy
    because of your great deeds.

Merciful God, how excellent
    are your works
    and how very deep are your thoughts.
The dull of heart do not understand.
Foolish minds do not comprehend.

Though wickedness flourishes
    and sin multiplies like roaches,
    they who follow evil ways
    breed their own destruction.
O Holy One, you are forever.
No evil can survive when you come near.

Great and gracious One,
    you fill my heart with delight.
You exalt my spirit in thanksgiving.
Each day you rescue me
    from my own foolishness.

Each moment, you hold me
    in the depths of your love.

The people who follow your ways
    will flourish like trees
    by an ever-flowing river.
They are like palms at a desert oasis
    which provide cooling shade
    in the heat of the day.
They are like a redwood forest
    standing tall in beauty and grace.

Great God, stay near your people,
    the people who are planted in your heart.
Stay close to those who live in your Spirit.
Honesty and patience are their garments.
They are shod with humility
    and belted with fidelity.
They are vested in truth and their cloak is love.
Kindness is their crown.
Even in old age, they shine with goodness.

Holy One, each one uniquely manifests
    your presence with us.
In You-Who-Are, we are secure!

93

Holy One, some people worship you
    as a God of power and might.
These feel secure with this idea.
And, yes, some worship you
    because of your power and might.
They do not treasure you at all.

Gracious One, some worship you
   as a God of glory and delight.
These, too, are satisfied with this image.
These simply enjoy the experience,
   the excitement and pleasure of worship.
They do not adore you at all.

Yahweh, you are Who-You-Are!
You are so much more
   than any idea or image can propose.
All existence emerges
   from your creative self.
Nothing continues to exist
   without your sustaining will.

Before all things were, You-Are.
Beyond all things,
You-Will-Always-Be.
You are steadfast to the covenant
you made with all creation.
You are faithful to the promises
   you gave to all humankind.

You are strong and true.
Nothing will change your gracious desire
   nor keep you from achieving
   the final fulfillment you have planned.
The winds may howl and the seas roar.
The lightning may flash and thunder roll.
The very earth may crumble into dust.
But your purposes will be accomplished.

Blessed be you, most Holy One,
   our eternal Guardian, Guide, and Friend.
Amen and amen.

94

Great and gracious One,
   you are a God of mercy and of mystery.
Let your mercy pour forth
   in an ever increasing torrent.
Let your mercy sweep away
   our stubborn blindness and sin.
Let us recognize you as Mystery
   for you remain, forever, beyond
   our ability to comprehend.

Holy and merciful One,
   you are a God of justice and of truth.
Let your justice grow
   in an ever increasing magnitude
   and let your truth prevail
   in every circumstance.

How long, O God, must your people suffer?
How long shall the proud
   walk in arrogance?
How long shall evildoers exult?

The wicked spout boastful words.
They treat the outcast with callous bigotry.
They afflict the helpless without scruple.
They murder the innocent without regret
   and trample the earth without restraint.
These immoral ones think
   that you do not see their deeds.
They ignore you and say you do not care.
Then they proclaim you do not exist.

Listen, you people who do evil!
When will you wake
   to wisdom and truth

The God who formed the earth
   does see.
The One who made you
   does care.
Yahweh teaches truth to the nations
   and imparts wisdom to the lowly.

Holy One, you know our thoughts.
Wake us to your wisdom.
Arouse us to your truth
Enkindle us to new life.

Happy the people who listen to Yahweh.
Blessed are the ones who learn God's ways.
These are the people who know inner peace
   even in the midst of many troubles.

O God, you are with your little ones.
You are with them in every moment.
You support your faithful ones
   through every affliction.
You do not abandon them.
Justice shall arise amid the peoples
   and equity among the nations.

O Holy One, your people
   will joyfully pursue your cause,
   while the wicked will fall into the pit
   that they made for themselves.

Gracious One, you comforted me.
Holy One, you helped me in my need.
If you had not aided me,
I would have died.
I knew I was falling
   and could do nothing.
Then your faithful love
   rescued and restored me.

You continue to give me solace
   when I am worn down with anxious care.
You come to me with gladness
   when I am flooded with misery.
You touch my inmost heart with joy.

Great God, you resist violence
   and reject corruption.
You bring unjust schemes to nothing.
You turn oppressors into dust
   and corrupt systems to naught.
The people who rule with injustice
   and maintain their power by force
   will fall by their own connivings.

You, great God, are my only security.
You are my rock of refuge in distress.
Wickedness shall perish
   while those who pursue the good
   are taken up into new life.

95

Come, O people!
Let us rejoice in our God.
Let us proclaim our gladness
to the One who loves us.
Let us go to Yahweh with gratitude.
Let us sing songs of thanksgiving
   to the Rock of our salvation.

For you, Yahweh, are our God.
You hold all creation
   in your tender embrace,
   from the farthest stars
   to the smallest atomic particles.

Out of your immense creative love,
    you form all things.
Nothing exists without you.
Come, O people!
Let us worship our God.
Let us bow down
    before the One who made us.
Yahweh, you are our God
    and we are your people.
We are your precious little ones.
We are your family,
    the ones whom you love.

Come, O people!
Listen today for Yahweh.
Open your heart to our God.
Do not be stubborn.
Do not let fear shut your ears.
Do not let shame blind your eyes.
Do not let guilt close your mind,
    for Yahweh aches to embrace you
    and longs to heal you.

Come, O people!
Let us rejoice in Yahweh.
Sing praise to our God. Alleluia!

96

Sing a new song to our God.
O let all the world sing
    to this immensely gracious Mystery.
Sing your gratitude and praise.
Proclaim the goodness
    of the One who made us.

Holy One, we tell of your gifts
   and rejoice in your blessings.
We declare the depths of your love.
We sing of your marvelous works
   among all the peoples.

Great God, day after day
   we rejoice in your saving power
   for you are the gracious One-Who-Is.

O peoples, reverence Yahweh
   above all things.
Love Yahweh before all else.

Yahweh, our God, is beyond peer.
Nothing equals God's beauty.
Nothing is above God's greatness.
Nothing approaches God's mercy.
Nothing matches God's goodness.
Everything else fades like smoke in the wind
   when compared to the One-Who-Is.

Our God created all things that are,
   all things that were,
   and all things that will be.
Yahweh sustains everything that exists.

Glory and graciousness
   go before our God.
Wisdom and fidelity
   enfold the One-Who-Is.
Mercy and healing
   flow from Yahweh's hands.
The heart of our God is flaming love
   and that love endures forever.

Praise God, all you peoples of the earth.
Rejoice in Yahweh's wondrous goodness.

Praise the One-Who-Is
   both light and truth.

Bring the offering of your heart
   into Yahweh's presence.
Bow down in gratitude and joy.
Let all the earth reverence our God.
Say to the world: Yahweh is supreme!

Holy One, you judge the peoples
   with equity.
You yearn for justice
   among the nations.
Nothing escapes your sight.

O heavens, be glad! O earth, rejoice!
Let the oceans rise in gratitude.
May all sea creatures give thanks.
Let the dry lands exult
   and every earth dweller give praise.
Let the forests sing for joy.
Let the mountains clap their hands
   before the One who made them.

The Holy One comes to judge the earth.
Yahweh judges the world with justice
   and all the peoples with equity.

97

Let the earth rejoice
   and the many isles be glad!
For you, great God, are the Creator
   of the cosmos and all it contains.

O God, you are the Sustainer
   of all that exists.
You are our Redeemer and Sanctifier.
And you are so great, so beautiful,
   our minds utterly fail to comprehend
   the wonder of Who-You-Are.
Holy One, you are beingness itself.
Our thoughts can not penetrate
   either your immediacy or fullness.
Our ideas can not follow
   either the height or depth or breadth
   of your encompassing purpose.

Gracious One, you are Mystery.
You are the Holy, wholly Other.
Yet you remain the firm foundation
   of all that exists.
Nothing comes to be outside of you.
All existence rests in you.

Trying to understand you is like
   trying to see in a pea-soup fog.
We grope to catch but a glimpse of you
   and make out only vague shapes in the gray.

Then, great God, without warning,
   as heat lightning, brightens the night sky,
   you illumine our awareness
   with your presence
   and we are interpenetrated with joy.
Our hearts melt like ice
   on a hot summer day
   and our souls are inebriated with delight.

O merciful Mystery,
   who can declare your glory?
What can convey the power
   of your holiness?

Who can speak the wisdom
   of your justice?
What can disclose the depths
   of your compassion?

Great God, the heavens proclaim your grandeur,
   and the peoples rejoice
   in your tender care.
The foolishness
   of chasing after things
   is revealed,
   and the stupidity of making things into gods
   is manifested.

Clearly you are God
   and there is no other.
Your little ones see and are glad.
All the oppressed
   lift up their hearts in joy.
All who are outcast
   are included with honor.
Because, O God, your judgments are true
   and your justice is mercy for all peoples.

You, great and gracious One,
   are the Most High over all the earth.
There is no God but you.
Your light shines on all the nations.
Your gladness fills the upright of heart.

O you peoples,
   bless and reverence our God.
Give thanks, you upright of heart,
   for Yahweh particularly rejoices
   in the people who choose good.
Yahweh watches over their lives
   and rescues them from evil.

Give thanks for what our God has done.
Remember the deeds of Yahweh.
Give thanks to our God, all you peoples.
Rejoice and give thanks forever.

98

O people fill the earth with joyful song.
Fill the air with melodies of thanksgiving,
  for Yahweh does wonderful deeds.

The earth is molded
  by Yahweh's awesome creativity.
The land is filled
  by Yahweh's infinite generosity.
Always and everywhere,
Yahweh's transforming love
  is revealed to all the nations.

O God, you keep your promises
  to all the inhabitants of the earth.
You show us your constant loyalty
  and fill us with your love.
The peoples of every nation
  will recognize your generous care.

Great God, we sing our joy to you.
All the earth sings melodies
  of gratitude and thanksgiving.
We rejoice in you
  and declare your goodness
  with shouts of praise.

Let the sea roar in worship
  and all creatures of the sea
  profess their praise.

Let the earth proclaim your glory
  and all who live upon dry land
  bow down in adoration.
Let the rivers sing their delight
  and all who live in their waters
  give thanks.
Let the mountains dance for joy
  and exalt the wonder of our God,
  for Yahweh is in our midst.
Our God creates justice for all peoples
  and equity among the nations.

Let everything that lives proclaim
  your greatness, O gracious One.

99

All you nations, worship Yahweh,
because Yahweh is the One-Who-Is.
All you peoples adore the Holy Mystery,
  for Yahweh is the creator and sustainer
  of all that exists.

You, O God, are the source of everything,
  and our hope of salvation.
You embrace earth's residents with mercy
  and judge the nations with impartiality.
You love justice and work unceasingly
  to establish right relations
  among all peoples.

Holy One, may all peoples reverence you.
May they praise
  and rejoice in You-Who-Are.
You are awesome and wonderful.

You are tender and compassionate.
You are mastery and Mystery.
We simply cannot fathom you.

In times past, many souls
looked to you and loved you.
They trusted you and followed your ways.
They cried out to you
   when they were in need.
You answered their call and rescued them.

O great God, you spoke to their hearts
   and, though you detest wrongdoing,
   still you were merciful.
You forgave their sins
   and turned their failures
   somehow to their good.

Holy One, you do the same for us.
You hear us and save us
   when we trust in you and follow you.
You hear us and save us
   when we turn to you in need.
You hear us and save us
   when we call on you in faith.

O God, continue to be merciful
   and forgive our sins.
Embrace us as we turn to you
   with contrite hearts.
You will turn our failures, somehow,
   into opportunities for good.

O most high and holy God,
   we exalt you with gratitude.
Help us to worship you
   in spirit and in truth.

Gracious One, you are
    ultimate glory and grandeur.
You are wonder and delight.
You are mercy and Mystery.
You are Yahweh, our God.
There is no other.

100

All you peoples, make a joyful noise
    before the One-Who-Is.
All the earth give thanks to our God.
Worship Yahweh with grateful song.
Acclaim the Holy One with joyful hearts.
Come into God's presence with praise.
Serve Yahweh with gladness.
    Know that Yahweh is God
    and God's mercy extends to all that exists.

Great God, you formed us and you know us.
We belong to you because you are our God.
We are your people,
    the flock you shepherd.
We are your faithful little ones,
    the people you hold close in your heart.

Come into God's house
    with thanksgiving.
Enter Yahweh's presence with praise.
Let us stand before the One-Who-Is
    with glad and grateful hearts.
Let us rejoice in this gracious Mystery.
Let us bless the Holy One
    with upraised hands.
For Yahweh's mercy is forever.

Your faithfulness, O God,
    flows forth to all peoples
    and your generous kindness
    extends to all generations.
May you be blessed,
    always and everywhere,
    through all generations,
    forever and ever.

101

Gracious God, I will sing
    of your abiding love.
I will proclaim your gracious mercy.
I will declare your glory and wisdom.
I will search for you
    and follow your paths.

Keep me from sin
    and save me from folly.
Keep my heart pure in every moment.
Do not let me fall into evil ways,
    and prevent me from turning away from you.
I so much need your constant aid
    for I am often blind and prone to sin.
Help me to be honest with myself
    and let me be honest with others.
Keep my tongue from speaking slander
    and my mouth from uttering lies.

Let my mind be intent on humble service.
And do not let my heart grow arrogant.
Help me to see you in the least
    of my brothers and sisters.
Show me the way to serve you in them.

May I continue to live in your presence
    with joyful heart and firm commitment.
Then morning by morning,
I will rejoice in your goodness
    and I will praise your mercy.
Then evening by evening,
I will declare your generosity
    and thank you for your loving kindness.
Because you are the God who loves me.

102

Great God, again I am lost in darkness.
Once more I am overcome with despair.
O God, listen to my pleading.
Holy One, hear my cry for help!
Do not abandon me in my need.
Answer me quickly for I am dying.

My life blows away
like smoke in the wind.
My body aches like fire.
I am beaten down and trampled,
like dry grass under every foot.
I cannot eat and do not sleep.
I groan aloud in my distress.

I am like a wild beast prowling the desert.
I am as an owl sitting among ruins.
I am as restless as a weather vane
    in a constantly changing wind.
All my efforts are dust.
All my hopes are ashes.
Tears are my food
    and anguish is my bitter drink.

My life is like an evening shadow
  slipping into night
  and, my God, you are so totally absent.
You are so very far away.

Come, Holy One, come!
Make your comforting presence
  known to me again.
Rise up and have compassion on me.

O God, have compassion
  on anyone crushed by woe.
Give hope and courage to everyone
  who clings to you.
Have pity on your little ones
  for you are our great and gracious God
  who loves and saves us.

Build up your people again.
Let them be as bright as a city on a hill.
Then they will draw others to your cause.
Then all the nations of the earth
  will reverence you.

The powerful will follow your desires
  and your justice will bring peace
  into the lives of all peoples.
Those who mourn shall laugh,
  and those who are destitute
  shall lack no good thing,
  for you have heard their cry
  and answered their need.

Great God, let your goodness show forth
  and your works be written for all to see.
Then generations yet to come
  will praise you with joy-filled hearts.

You are not far off,
    but rather, you are near.
You are never absent,
    but always present to every creature.
You hear the groans of prisoners
    and the cries of those who are ensnared.
You free transgressors from their sins
    and loose the captives from their bonds.
You give new life to all who call upon you.

You will be exalted by all the peoples
    while those who love you
    sing glad songs of praise,
    for the nations are gathered in peace
    and justice rules the earth.

But my strength is gone.
My hope flickers like a dying candle.
O my God, save me!
You-Who-Are forever,
    reach out and catch me!

You created the universe
    and all that is in it.
Moment by moment and day by day,
    you hold all things in being.

Yet each person lives but a few years
    and all things cease to be
    at their appointed time.
Though people perish
    and things are no more,
you endure, great God, you endure.

All creation eventually wears out
    like a well-used garment.
Like last year's leaves,
    we too return to the earth.

But, Yahweh, You-Always-Are.
You are beingness itself.
You have no beginning and no end.
So in you, gracious One,
    your little ones are established.
The people who are rooted in you
    are protected through all generations.
Your servants rest secure.
No affliction shall disturb them anymore.

103

Bless Yahweh, O my soul!
Let all my being bless the gracious One.
Praise our God, O my spirit,
    and remember all Yahweh's kindnesses.

You, gracious One,
    forgive all iniquities.
You heal every disease.
You create each thing
    at its assigned time.
You sustain everything
    for its appointed term.
You fill my life with good.
From all eternity
I am blessed by love.
Daily these good gifts are given,
    pressed down
    and running over.

Bless Yahweh, O my soul!
Let all my being
    bless the gracious One.

Great and generous One,
   you are especially mindful
   of the oppressed.
You favor the voiceless
   and stand with the powerless.
You hear the cry of the persecuted
   and enfold the helpless
   in your tender embrace.

You showed your concern through Moses.
You revealed your deepest desire
   through the people of Israel.
They were voiceless and powerless,
   persecuted and helpless,
   and you set them free from slavery.
You led them into a new life,
   a life flowing with milk and honey.

Holy One, you are mercy and love.
You are forgiveness and new beginnings.
You do not abandon your people.
You do not forget your care.
Enduring compassion is your name.

We may stumble and fall.
We may fail you many times.
But you are always there
   to pick us up and dust us off.
You put us back on our feet
   and tell us to keep trying.

As wide as this universe, and beyond,
   your love flows out for all your creation.
As far as the farthest star and farther still,
   you place any memory of our failures.
As parents hover over their children
   and desire only the best for their offspring,
   so Yahweh is mindful of all creation.

O God, you know how we are made.
You remember how limited
   and weak we are.
Our lives are short and quickly pass.
We are like the morning mist
   that vanishes as the sun rises
   or a puff of smoke that disappears
   as it climbs into the sky.
We are here and then we are gone.

Still, Yahweh, you are forever.
Your love is eternal,
   and your goodness endures
   through all generations.
But many still cling
   to false images of you.
Some see you only
   as an awesome God
   of power and might.
Many others see you only
   as a harsh God of
   anger and vengeance.

Still others desire
   your promised rewards
   more than they desire
   your presence,
   your work,
   or your will.
They seek a place of authority
   and admiration.
These put you on a throne
   and call you king.
These envision a throne for themselves
   and the power to legislate over others.
They do not recognize you as servant,
   nor understand you as faithful friend.

Some people also proclaim
    a punitive God.
O God, such people take secret delight
    in stories of sinners
    tossed into outer darkness
    while they, of course, are secure
    as they sit with Jesus on their thrones.

How constricted are these visions.
How distorted these ideas.
Whoever holds them does not see.
These images are human feelings
    written large upon a blank screen
    they call God.
These are human desires
    projected onto infinity in limitless folly.

But how happy are they
    who humbly seek to know you.
How blessed are they
    who keep near to you in their hearts.
How precious are they
    who follow your way of mercy and care
    for all your creation.

Bless Yahweh, all creation.
Bless the Holy One,
    you who do God's will.
Let both great and small
    bless this gracious Mystery
    now and forever.

104

Rejoice in Yahweh, O my heart!
Give thanks to Yahweh, O my soul!

Holy One, you are great indeed!
You make yourself known
    throughout the cosmos.
Your originality is awesome.
The whole universe proclaims
    your magnificent creativity.
This little planet manifests
    your extravagant fruitfulness.

Holy One, you are great indeed!
You bring everything into existence.
You weave each quark and glue-on
    into its proper spot and moment.
You place each microbe and midge,
plant, animal, and person,
    in its rightful place and time.

Holy One, you are great indeed!
The heavens manifest your glory
    and this planet is your cherished pearl.
You are the sure foundation of this earth.
Each moment you hold our world in being.
As a mother tenderly holds her little child,
    so you tenderly hold this tiny planet.

Gracious One, you are great, indeed!
You are like the primal seas
    who gave birth to all life in this world.
Earth's immense oceans
    symbolize the vastness of your love.
These oceans' multitudinous life forms
    suggest the breadth of your designs.

The mysteries of their deeps
   signify the unfathomed depths
   of the Mystery of you.

Generous One, you are great indeed!
You are like the fruitful earth,
   stable and secure, providing for our needs.
Mountain ranges stand like sentinels
   telling of your grandeur,
   and verdant valleys proclaim your care.
Clouds and winds become your messengers.
Rain and sun come in your service.
Summer, fall, winter, and spring
   come as your ministers.

Merciful One, you are great indeed!
You manifest yourself in quiet springs
   and rushing rivers.
You show yourself through every life form.
You are seen in the immense varieties
   of trees and flowers
   and in every kind of plant.

You are glimpsed in all creeping things.
Sea creatures play in your embrace.
The birds of the air are enfolded
   in your care.
Everything speaks of your benevolence.
All life reveals your wondrous power.
In you all living things find a home
   and each uniquely declares your glory.

Holy God, you are great indeed!
You are the Source and Sustainer of life.
In the great cycle of birth and death,
you are actively present.
You are there in birth
   and in new beginnings.

You bring forth new life
   in each moment and circumstance.

You are there at death
   and final dissolution.
And you walk with all beings
through death into a new existence.
You create new beginnings from the dust.
Nothing good is ever lost in you.

Great God, how wonderful are your works!
How marvelous the revelation
   of Who-You-Are in them.
With wisdom you create each and all.
Through wisdom your glory is proclaimed.
Rain falls to earth from the clouds
   and the earth is filled with your blessings.
Plants grow and sustain the animals.
You provide food for each creature
   in due season.
All eat and are satisfied.

Crops grow and provide food
   for humankind.
Wheat and rice and beans,
   potatoes and corn,
   are cultivated to nourish human life.
Meat and fish add relish to any repast.
Eggs and oil add satisfaction to a meal.
Fruits, nuts, spices, and green vegetables
   bring savory textures and flavors;
   while milk, wine and beer add cheer.

May you be glorified in all you create.
May you be pleased with everything
   you bring to be.
May you rejoice in earth and sea and sky
   and in every creature under heaven.

May all creation sing praise to you
    in all their multitude of forms and kinds.

I will sing to you, most gracious One.
As long as I live, I will rejoice in you.
I will give you thanks every day of my life.
May this prayer be pleasing to you
    who are my hearts blood.
Let all who wander far from you
    be brought safely home.
May each be touched by your mercy
    and transformed by your love.

Rejoice in God, O my soul.
Gracious One, you are great indeed!

105

How great you are, most loving One.
How good, how marvelous your ways.

You make yourself known
    among the peoples.
You are known in your words
    and in your works.
Happy the people who take you
    to be their God.
They shall sing in joyful praise.

Seek the One who is wisdom and mercy.
Remember God's good works.
Remember Yahweh's marvelous miracles
    and the Holy One's righteous judgments.

O peoples of this earth,
     you are God's chosen.
You are Yahweh's beloved.
The Holy One will not abandon you.
The One-Who-Is has sworn fidelity.
God has promised to love us forever
     in an everlasting covenant for all ages.

For from time before remembrance,
     Yahweh brooded over the void.
Then out of the fireball of creation
     God formed the universe.
From the dust of that making,
     God shaped the stars.

For more eons than can be imagined,
God carried this little planet,
     molten and desolate,
     as a mother carries a child in her womb.
Thus Yahweh labored to birth this earth.
The Most High gently embraced this globe
     and declared it was very good.

And in the fullness of time
God brought forth teaming life
     on this planet.
Yahweh blessed these living things
     and generously cared for all of them.
Yahweh loved each and every one
     and declared they were very good.

Out of this abounding life,
God formed a self-reflective being,
     a being who had the capacity to mirror
     Yahweh's own heart.
The Holy One blessed this creation.
Our gracious Mystery loved humanity
     and declared that we were very good.

But like an infant which stumbles and falls
   as the child learns to walk
   so people made mistakes.
Their missed steps were compounded.
Their mistakes were blended with fear.
Missed steps were mixed with envy.
Mistakes challenged mastery
   and self reliance.
Fear combined with anger.

Instead of connection,
   people felt separation.
Instead of affirmation,
   people felt condemned.
So, feeling separated
   and lost in their own eyes,
   sin entered the world.
The dread of death soon followed.

People were afraid of those
   who were different.
They denounced views and customs
   which were not their own.
This apprehension generated hate.
Oppression arrived soon after.

People coveted others' possessions.
Murder entered the land.
The desire for revenge sprouted.
Soon tribe rose against tribe
   and nation against nation.
Sins multiplied
   and the image of a merciful God,
   was lost to awareness.

People made gods
   in their own worst images:
   capricious, jealous, and angry.

These gods must be placated
    with mighty sacrifices to appease anger.
They must be served with abject fear
    to turn disaster from the door.

But the compassionate One
    did not turn away from humanity.
A loving Creator did not abandon
    this foolish, fear-filled creature.

Again and again,
Yahweh raised up persons
    who made the Holy One's love
    manifest through their actions
    and God's mercy visible
    through their attitudes.
Yahweh raised up individuals
    who spoke of God's gracious goodness
    to a misguided and hurting world.
Yahweh called forth faithful people
    and raised up honest people;
Yahweh supported compassionate people
    to image the good,
    communicate the true,
    and reveal the Holy One's
    loving care for this world.

And Yahweh began to form
    a particular people.
These people were called
    to grow in knowledge and love of God.
They were to make God's love
    visible to all peoples.
They were meant to demonstrate
    God's plan to save humanity from itself.

This group was not the greatest
    nor the best of earth.

They were few in number
   and of little account.
In the sweep of human history,
   they were wanderers on this planet.

Slowly, over centuries,
God taught them.
Over and over, Yahweh rescued them.
Again and again they were brought back
   when they got lost in sin.
The gracious One dispelled ignorance
   and cast out fear.
God preserved them
   when they were crushed
   by war and deceit and folly.

The Holy One did great things for them.
Yahweh brought them into the land
   that had been promised to them.
Thus Yahweh's faithfulness
   was shown to all.
God's tender care was made clear
   to every generation.

Through priests and prophets,
   national leaders and humble servants,
God kept the light of love
   and the truth of God's care
   alive in the world.

Then, in the fullness of time,
Yahweh's universal love
   and faithfulness became visible
   in the man called Jesus.
Jesus was completely human,
   yet remains the totally authentic image
   of You-Who-Are, great God.

Thus Jesus is the definitive disclosure
   of your extravagant love for everyone.
Jesus is the authoritative sign
   of your tender concern for all creation.
You tenderly embrace every mote
   and moment of this wonderful cosmos.

Gracious One, Jesus is the revelation
   of Your-presence-with-us.
He clearly speaks your word
   of truth and justice.
He shows us your endless mercy.
He demonstrates your will for our good
   and the well being of every creature.
Holy God, Jesus shines with your beauty.
It is the beauty of your love for all people.
Those who hear his message
   are brought out of fear and into joy.

Loving One, those who accept his gift
   know your love and live your truth.
They know, with surety and joy,
   the truth of your connection
   with all humanity.
They know the truth of their connection
   with every other person
   and all things on this planet.

Merciful One, they celebrate your love
   for all of your creation.
And because you are the trusted center
   of their lives, they are free from fear.
Because they know, deep down,
   your infinite care for them,
   they are free to care for others.
Seeing the interdependence among all creatures,
   they are inspired to work for greater justice
   amid all living things.

Singing with gratitude,
   they are filled with a peace
   that cannot be taken away.

Great and gracious Mystery,
   how happy are they who know you.
How joyful the people who see your heart.
How infinite is your goodness
   toward all your creation.
How mighty your compassion
   for everything that exists.
How wonderful are the depths of your love.

We praise you, most loving One!
With awe-struck gratitude,
   may we praise you forever.

106

We exult in you, most gracious God.
We rejoice in you, for you are good.
We thank you, for your love endures forever.

Who can know all the things you have done?
Who can speak the number of your gifts?
Who can say the extent of your blessings?
Who can declare enough praise
   for the multitude of your great works?
Happy are the people who pursue justice.
Happy are they who always do what is right.

Remember us, O gracious God.
Remember us and reach out to help us
   reach out to us for we are your people.

Help us all and save us from our sins.
Assist us so we may know
 the blessings you have promised
 to those who follow your paths.
Support everyone who follows your ways
 so they may know your mercy and love.

May you, Holy One, have great joy
 in the prosperity of your people.
May you be pleased by the fidelity
 of your chosen ones.

Still, Holy One, we so frequently fail you.
Gracious One, we so often sin against you.
We so repeatedly forget
 that our own well being
 is rooted in following you.
We do not remember your vast mercy.
 and do not recall your loving kindness.

So, like the people before us,
 we stray from you.
We prefer to stay in our darkness
 rather than live in your wonderful light.
We refuse to accept your infinite love for us.
Instead, we cling to our self centered desires.
We hold fast to our hurtful attitudes
 toward others and misshaped ideas of you.

As our ancestors forgot them,
 so we forget your saving graces.
We do not remember the many times
 you have rescued and renewed us.
Again, we forget your gracious goodness:
 poured out to overflowing.

Again and again, you save us from disaster.
Over and over, you open a way to new life.

Time after time, you reach out to us,
  saying: Do not fear little flock,
  for I am with you
  to comfort you and give you strength.

Gracious One, help us to believe!
Help us to accept your acceptance of us.
Help us to really trust your steadfast love
Help us to sing praise for Who-You-Are.

But still we continue to forget
  your saving power and your loving kindness.
We grumble and fear.
We chase after will-o'-the-wisps.
We deny your presence and mock your love.
We remain fools, calling ourselves wise.
We still chain ourselves to sins.
We fail to see your steadfast love.

Holy One, you want to save us
  and bring us back to you.
Help us to really appreciate
  your generosity and kindnesses.
May we be truly grateful
  for all your blessings.

Most loving One, we praise you!
Most glorious One, we thank you.
Let everyone give praise to you.
Let all the peoples shout: alleluia and amen!
Most gracious and merciful One,
  may the praise and the glory be yours,
  always and everywhere, now and forever.

107

Most high and glorious God,
  we praise you and give you thanks.
  for your mercy endures forever.

Let all who live proclaim their gratitude.
Let each whom you have saved.
  give thanks to you.
Let everyone whom you have rescued
  declare their praise.
Let those whom you freed from dark places
  profess their eternal gratitude.
Let the ones whom you liberated
  shout their joy.
Let each whom you returned
  to an honored place in the human family
  offer homage to your goodness.

For, great God,
  we were fainting from hunger
  and you fed us.
We were staggering from thirst
  and you gave us to drink.
We had lost our way when you found us
  and brought us back to you.

When we were perishing,
  we cried out to you
  and you lifted us from our distress.
You led each of us by a straight path
  until we reached safety.
You revived our failing spirits
  and restored us to health.
You continue to carry each of us
  close to your heart.

Let all give you thanks
   for your enduring love,
   for the wonderful works that you do.
You fill the hungry
   and satisfy the thirsty.
You heal the wounded
   and restore the weak.
You comfort the sorrowful
   and give peace to the afflicted.

Gracious One, we sat in darkness
   because we would not listen to you.
We had turned away from your counsels
   and our hearts were filled with fear.
We were prisoners of misery
   and victims of despair.
We were crushed, with no one to help.

Then, Most High, we cried out to you.
We sought you in the midst of our troubles.
We turned to you in our distress
   and, wonder of wonders, you saved us.
You brought us out of darkness.
You set us free from fear.
So, Most High, we rejoice in you.
We proclaim your steadfast love.
We thank you for your wonderful works.
We celebrate your healing power.
We bless you for helping us
   and bringing us home to you.

Though some are still foolish
   and follow sinful ways,
   these blindly suffer the consequences of their actions.
Yet they can still cry out to you
   and you will always save them.
Your wisdom/word goes out
   and you deliver them from destruction.

O God, we declare your gracious deeds
   with songs of joy.
We are so grateful for your abiding care.
We thank you for your wonderful works
   and rejoice in your healing touch.
We bless you for helping us
   and bringing us home to you.

Great God, we go about our normal lives.
We eat and sleep
   and make plans for the day.
Some journey by land.
Others go by sea.
Many more travel by air.
We each pursue our own desires.

But when storms come into our lives,
   we are tossed about
   like tiny boats on tumultuous seas;
   or we are buffeted like small planes
   by the roiling winds of a turbulent sky;
   and human courage melts away
   like ice on a summer day.

Then, in our terror,
   we turn to you, Most High.
In our distress, we cry out for help
   and, wonder of wonders,
   you rescue and renew us.
You calm the stormy waves
   and we are glad because the danger is gone.
You turn the winds to zephyrs
   and we are grateful because we are safe.

O God, we give thanks to you
   and praise your compassionate love.
Holy One, may we rejoice in you
   in the midst of the people.

Let us proclaim Yahweh's goodness
in the assembly of the nations.

Most High and Holy One,
You watch over your people.
You are close to each and every person,
no matter what their circumstances.
You weep for those who have gone astray.
You are deeply saddened by those
who make a wasteland of their lives.
You hound them from their depths.
and they know no peace
until they turn to you.
But, with joy, you make yourself known
to those who seek you.
You fill with immense gladness
those who follow your ways.
You support them.
You encourage them.
You give great peace to anyone
who does you will.

You rejoice in the people
who help the vulnerable.
You celebrate those
who free the oppressed.
You carry humble folk carefully,
in your heart.
Out of every situation
You bring good to your people.
You bless each and rejoice in each
and lead each one safely home.
You raise the needy from the dust
and lift the despised from the trash heap.

Your people see this and are glad.
Let wise people give heed to these words
and consider Yahweh's steadfast love.

108

O God, my heart is glad in you.
I sing your praise and give you thanks.
When I wake in the morning, I praise you.
My heart sings melodies of happy gratitude.

Great God, I thank you!
I thank you every moment of every day.
I rejoice in you among your people
I praise you for the people I know
   and for the people I will know
   and for those I will never know,
   but you know in your abiding love.
You are enduring compassion.
Your care for us is faithful and eternal.

Let the glory of your greatness
   be seen by the nations.
Let the depth of your generosity
   be revealed to every people.
By the saving power of your love,
   rescue all of us.
In the immensity of your wisdom,
   renew each of us.
Bring peace to our earth
   and tranquility to every human heart.

Gracious God, speak your word of peace
   in the depths of our hearts.
Say to the tumult of this world: Peace!
Say amid the noise of our minds:
Be still! And know that I am God!
Say in the depths of our souls:
Fear not! I love you!
Say to our anxious hearts:
   You are my beloved little ones!

Come and partner me.
Come and be my companions.
Come and help me to reclaim this earth
and renew all things.

Holy God, how deep our gratitude will be
when we really hear your words.
How great our joy will be
when we move to act on them.

Who, merciful God, will speak
of your magnanimous gifts?
Who will manifest your surging love
to our hurting world?

You have the final word.
You will never stop caring.
You will never stop forgiving.
You will never stop creating.
You will never stop rescuing
until your purposes are accomplished
and all things are made new.
Nothing can deflect you from your course.
Nothing will stop the final fulfillment
of your desires.

109

Gracious One, how great you are
and how wonderful.
How mighty are your deeds of power.
How glorious your generosity.

Yet I am beset and harried.
People plot against me
and say evil things about me.

They attack me for no reason.
Though I am kind to them
and pray for their good,
they repay me with evil,
and return hatred for the good
that I do for them.

What is wrong with us, O God?
Why do we despise and attack one another?
What makes us prefer meanness to kindness?
Why do we seek darkness rather than light?
What drives us to hatching evil schemes
and plotting violence against one another?
Why do we impose misery on each other
generation after generation?

O God, we deserve to be lost.
We ought to be forgotten
every time we are not kind to someone,
each time we persecute and despise another,
when we turn away from those in need
whenever we curse others,
when we try to silence and even kill
those who disagree with us.
We are indeed enemies to each other.
We are totally separated from you.
We sit shrouded in dreadful darkness
and are headed toward complete despair.

Yet, great and gracious One,
out of your abundant goodness,
turn us once more to you.
In your infinite mercy,
forgive our sins
and help us to forgive those
who sin against us.

Rescue us, Compassionate One!

Because of your steadfast love,
  help us as you promised.
We need your saving gift,
  though some know it not.
We need your healing,
  though some deny it.
We ask your life and your love
  to infuse us
  and bring us home.

O God, thank you, for you hear our prayer.
How great you are and how wonderful!

110

Yahweh, you spoke thus
  to your wisdom/word:
Come, take your place,
  a place of highest honor,
  while I put all things into your hands.

From Jerusalem, I send forth my mercy.
From Zion, I spread out my compassion.
You shall overcome all resistance.
Everyone shall acclaim you with joy.

Glory is yours at your birth.
Like dew appears before the dawn,
I have begotten you.
I have sworn and will not repent:
  you are with me for all eternity.
You will always be with me,
  as I am always with you.
You are my call, extended for all peoples,
  to lead lives of loving service.

As I am, so you will be!
I prepare the way for you.
Nothing shall prevent
   the completion of my plan.

My judgment is mercy upon all flesh.
From a brook by the wayside
I shall give refreshment.
Therefore the poor will give thanks
   and the oppressed lift up their heads.

111

I thank you, O God, with all my heart.
I praise you in the assembly,
   with all your people.

How wonderful are your works!
We delight in remembering them.
We seek to understand your way.
All you do is full of grace.
Your glory overflows
   and your mercy is forever.

Holy One, you do not forget your people.
You are always mindful of your creation.
All your actions toward us are kind.
They are generous beyond measure.
You show your goodness to all humankind
   and you hold those who reverence you
   with special joy.
You provide for the needs
   of all your creatures:
      food and drink, and a place to rest.

You never forget your promises.
You are faithful in all your words
    and just in all your works.
We can trust you without limit
We can believe in you without reserve.
Your promises last forever.

You are truth and righteousness.
You are mercy and forgiveness of sin.
You set people free from fear
You bring peace to every creature.

You made an eternal covenant with us.
Holy and wonderful are you!
Wisdom and reverence go before you.
    and prudent judgment follows.
We praise you, O God!

112

Yahweh, happy are they who trust in you.
Happy are they who delight in your words.
How blessed are they
    who are careful to follow your ways.

Their lives are filled with joys.
They are rich with many blessings.
Their good influence is handed down
    from generation to generation.
Their lives are taken up in you.
They will endure forever.

Though events are sometimes trying
    and arduous problems abound,
        these are people of justice and mercy.

They are people of compassion and courage.
They are a light for the peoples
    of this world.
They manifest your presence, Holy One,
    for all to see

Like you, great God,
    they are gracious and merciful.
They build up justice for all peoples.
The give freely to the poor.
Their kindness never fails.
These are honored in the assembly
    and respected by the community.
Those who generously lend
    and conduct their affairs with honesty
    will live with assurance all their lives.

Through joy and sorrow
    they are not afraid.
There is meaning and purpose
    in their life.
Their hearts are secure in you, great God.
Their hearts are secure in you.

113

Praise, O friends and lovers of our God,
    praise the One-Who-Is, forever.
Blessed be Yahweh, both now and always.
From the rising of the sun to its setting
    may the Holy One be praised.

Our God is not like any created thing.
Who is like the One-Who-Is?

What can compare to our God,
   the Creator, who encompasses
   the heavens and the earth.
Yahweh can be imaged
   but never fully understood.
Yahweh is a glorious Mystery.

Yet God raises the needy from the dust
   and lifts the poor from the garbage dump
   to places of recognition and respect.
God makes fruitful the barren wastes.
Yahweh creates a joyful dwelling place
   for all the little ones of the Most High.

114

O God, you reach out to us
   and we awaken to you.
You touch us and we are healed.
You call us and we turn to you.
You teach us and we come to know you.
You did this in ancient times
   and you do it for us now.

Let the seas rise up and roar in joy.
Let the rivers dance their praise.
Let the streams burble thanksgiving
   and springs flow out in gratitude.

Let the mountains jump and run
   like carefree children.
Let the hills proclaim your glory.
Let the whole earth be pregnant
   with your presence
   giving birth to new beginnings.

Come, O God! Awaken us.
Once more touch and heal us.
Once more turn us to you.
Once more teach us your ways.
    For you are our God.

You are our rock of safety.
You are our salvation,
    flowing out to all generations.
Come, O spring of living water!
Come, O Life Divine!
Come to us now!

115

Not to us, Holy One, not to us,
    but to you alone be the honor,
    because of your enduring love.
Not to us, great God, not to us,
    but may you alone be reverenced,
    for the sake of your abiding care.

The nations that do not know you,
    the peoples who follow after other gods
    say to us: Where is your God?

Gracious One, you are everywhere.
Yet you remain beyond all things.
You do as you wish
    and what you wish is always
    and everywhere
    the good of all your creation.

Yet money is the god of countless persons.
And power is the god of many more.

The god of others is named prestige.
These are human gods.
They spring from the human heart.
When their followers die
    these gods disappear for them.

Security is the god of myriad people.
Comfort is the god of countless more.
But, there is never enough security.
There is no permanent assurance,
    and comfort is never perfect.

So these gods, too,
    give no lasting satisfaction
In time, they also crumble into dust.
Some make a god of their nation
    or their tribe or their race.
Some make a political movement
    or philosophical idea into their god.
Still more make their body into their god.
They seek nothing but to please their senses.
These gods, too, will return to the earth.

For some, their god is a good reputation.
For others, their god is simply fame.
They want recognition
    for their face and name.
These people have also all gone astray

May those who trust in these gods
    see the futility of pursuing them.
O Yahweh, may they turn to you.
May they know the truth.
    and be transformed.

Trust in Yahweh,
    all you peoples of the earth.
The holy One helps and protects you.

Trust in Yahweh, the One-Who-Is.
Yahweh, our God, helps and protects us.
Yahweh remembers and blesses us.
Yahweh is ever mindful of all creation.

O God, may you bless your people.
May you bless everyone who honors you,
    both small and great.
May Yahweh give peace and joy
    to you and your children.
May you be totally fulfilled
    by the Holy One,
    the God who made the heavens
    and the earth.
All creation is held in the heart
    of this Holy Mystery.
Yahweh gives humanity
    stewardship over the earth.

O God, those who are lost in sin
    do not praise you.
You are not honored
    by those who choose evil.
But we who love and revere you
    will give you thanks,
    now and forever.

116

I love you, O my God.
You heard my cry to you
    and you listened to me.
I love you, O my God.
So again I turn to you for help.
Once more, I call upon you for aid.

I will sing songs of praise to you
    from morning to night.
I will proclaim my gratitude
    all my days.
I was about to die.
Death was standing at my door.
I was wracked with distress.
Anguish held me in its grip.
Then I called out to you, my God.
I cried: Oh God, save my life!
And you rescued me.

Great God, you are so generous.
You are kind and merciful.
You protect the innocent.
The humble you do not spurn.
You saved me when I was very low.
Return, oh my soul, to your tranquility.

My God, you delivered me from death.
You freed my eyes from tears
    and kept my feet from stumbling.
I still walk in your presence
    in the land of the living.

Gracious One, I trusted in you
    even when I was crushed.
I believed in you
    even when I was afraid,
I said: Holy One, what can I give you
    for your great goodness?
I will lift up the cup of gratitude.
I will raise a cup in thanksgiving
    for my salvation.
I will perform my promises to you
    in the assembly of all the people.

Most High, I remain your servant.
I am a member of your household.

You saved me from death.
How precious in your sight
   is the faithfulness of your little ones,
      even unto death, O God, even unto death.

I will raise a cup of thanksgiving
   and offer you my prayer of praise.
I will perform my promises to you
   in the company of all your people.
I will fulfill my vows to you
   in the assembly of your followers.

117

We praise you, O God.
Let all the nations praise you.
We thank you, O God.
Let the whole earth sing gratitude.
We adore you, O God.
Let all the peoples worship you.
For great is your love,
   and greater still, your steadfast care.
Your faithfulness endures forever.

Your word brings forth in due season
   everything that exists.
Your wisdom sustains all things
   in their places.
You are present to every generation.
You created all things
   and you sustain each in being.
Nothing is lost from your sight.
Gracious One, come and complete
   what you have started.

Every person struggles with afflictions.
Each encounters confusions,
    dilemmas, and paradoxes.
Everyone endures many sufferings.
All know fears and failures.
Weaknesses entrap us.

Because we are human,
    we need your wisdom.
Free us from fear and folly!
We depend on you for support.
We look to you for encouragement.
We ask your strength and courage
in every moment and circumstance.

Great God, justice and mercy
    are your garments.
Wisdom is your glory.
I seek your wisdom.
I ask your mercy.
I look for the good,
    for the good of our world.

Your wisdom is wiser
    than all our gathered knowledge.
You grant deeper understandings
    than all that our sciences
    and philosophies can teach.

Gracious One, I rejoice in recalling you
    at each moment of the day.
How sweet are your words to my tongue.
You are sweeter than honey to my soul.
Your word is a light that guides my feet.
Your wisdom is a lamp that lights my path.
Your wisdom/word is a beacon to my eye
    and a fire igniting my spirit.

Holy One, my life is in your care.
Though at times I feel besieged
    and sometimes depressed,
I will always cling to you.
You are my heritage forever.
You are the joy of my heart.
I hope in you alone.

Generous One, you are wonderful!
Therefore my spirit keeps watch for you.
Your words bestow true knowledge.
They give understanding to the humble.

Great God, you are righteousness itself
    and your righteousness is your mercy.
Your judgments are true.
Your compassion is complete.
It is poured out on all generations.

My heart is afire with zeal for your cause.
My soul is thirsty for justice in our world.
But I am small and of little account.
I cannot affect the actions of nations.
I cannot sway the powerful.
I have no influence on the great.
Yet I long for the coming of your kin-dom.

Merciful One, save us all!
Preserve us according to your steadfast love.
Have mercy so that all of us may live.
The whole of your word is truth.
Thus you declare: All things work to the good
    of those that love you.

My soul rests in your presence.
I seek you with all my heart.
All my ways are before you.
Peace is your gift to those who love you.

They do not err, who follow your way.
Deliver me, according to your great mercy.

Let me praise you while I live
   and let your gentle hand always guide me.
When I stumble lift me up,
   and when I stray seek me out
   for I do not forget you.
O God, I do love you!
Amen and amen.

118

We thank you, great God,
   for you are good,
    and your mercy endures forever.

Let all the peoples of the earth declare:
Your mercy endures forever.
Let the inhabitants of our land declare:
Your mercy endures forever.
Let everyone who reverences you declare:
Your mercy endures forever.
From out of the depths, I called to you.
You answered me and rescued me.

Gracious One, you are always with me.
Why should I fear?
Holy One, you are always with me.
What can cause me harm?

O God, it is better to put my trust in you
   than to put my faith in people.
It is better to take refuge in you
   than to put my belief in technology.

Holy One, troubles surrounded me.
Yet with your help, O God, I escaped them.
The problems seemed overwhelming,
    but you, gracious One, came to my aid.

O God, you are my strength
    and my courage.
You have become my salvation.
There are glad songs of gratitude
    in the hearts of those who love you.

The word of Yahweh does great deeds.
The wisdom of Yahweh has raised me up.
Yahweh does wondrous works.
Most gracious One, I shall not die,
    but live and tell of your mighty deeds.

Open to me the gates of justice
    and I will enter them.
I will give you thanks, my God.
I will rejoice in you
    because you answered me
    and have become my savior.

O God, this is the day
    that you have made.
Let us rejoice and be glad in it.
The stone rejected by the builders
    has become the cornerstone.
This is Yahweh's doing.
It is wonderful in our eyes.

Holy One, grant us your light
    and we shall be renewed.
Blessed are all who come
    in your love, O God.
We bless you with all our hearts.
Yahweh, the High and Holy One,
    is our God.

O God, you give us life and light.
Therefore we are joyous
   and make merry before you.
Yahweh, you are my God;
I praise you and give you thanks.
I exalt in you with my whole being.

Holy One, may all praise you.
May all thank you, for you are good
   and your mercy endures forever.

119

All who are open to you, O God, are happy.
The ones who seek to know you are blessed.
The people who trust in you
   shall be vindicated.
They who search for you
   with all their hearts shall find their desire.

Beloved are they, O God.
They are embraced by your love
   and they love in return.
They do no wrong
   because they are deeply aware
   of their connection to all things in you
   and the unity of everything in you.

Caring One, you repeatedly proved
   your care for us.
You diligently showed us your love.
You steadfastly pursued us with your mercy.
You fixed your kindly gaze on each of us.

Draw me, O God, ever more deeply
    into your presence.
I seek you with my whole heart.
Bring me ever more fully into your love
and keep me totally turned toward you.
I treasure your presence with me.
I delight in the word you speak to me.
I cherish your wisdom poured into my soul.

Each day I will bless you, most loving One.
Blessed be you, most gracious One!
Teach me your paths and lead me.
With my lips I will declare
    your wondrous goodness.
With my mouth I will proclaim
    your marvelous care.
I choose your way of faithfulness.
I cling to your presence
    for you are my God and my All.

Faithful are you, O God.
I will not forget your kindnesses.
You are a steadfast companion.
You are a true friend.
I will seek for nothing but you
    for all my life.

Gracious are you, my God.
I am intoxicated by your wisdom.
I meditate on your precepts
    and your word is ever before me.
I delight in your ways,
    more than in anything else in the world.

Holy One, be gentle with me.
Help me to live in you as you live in me.
Open my heart to see the wonders
    of your creative powers.

Your words are my delight.
Your precepts are my counselors.
Even when I sit in darkness
    and my soul wanders in gloom,
I will meditate on your goodness
    and proclaim your faithful love.

I trust your word to me.
Do not take your presence from me.
My only hope is in you.
I will trust in you always.
I am resolved to love you forever.
I shall walk freely in your company.
I will speak of your kindness
    to those whom you send to me.
I shall not falter in declaring your goodness.

Justice is my delight
    and mercy is my inheritance.
O God, let your steadfast love lead me.
Keep me true to your commands.
Help me to embrace your cause.
Rouse me to consider another's need.
Keep me from seeking selfish gain.

Keep my hope in you, great God.
Remember me in your compassion.
You are my comfort in distress.
I turn to you and I am consoled.
I think of your love and find strength.
I look to you and know courage.

Let your faithful care fulfill every need.
Let your saving power lift each soul.
You are my melody in the day.
You are my song in the night.
I remember you on my bed
    and keep your presence always before me.

My delight is in you, O God.
My whole being desires you.
It is only you whom I love.
Let the fire of this love grow and grow!
You are my all consuming joy.
Your promises are true.
Your presence is everlasting.
You are Fullness of Life.
This blessing you give to me.
O God, you are my truth and my life.
You are my delight and my peace.

Nothing will keep me from following you.
When I meditate on your ways,
I turn my feet to your paths.
When I think of your precepts,
I hurry to follow them.
I rise at midnight to praise you.
I am up at dawn to give you thanks.
I rejoice in the company
of those who love you.
I am grateful for the example
   of those who follow your ways.

Oft times, though, I am distracted
   and sometimes snared by failures.
I do not forget your love.
Remembering your care
   draws me from disaster
   and returns me to you.
Your mercy gives me new life
   and brings new beginnings.

Put your hand out, Holy One,
   when I go astray.
It is good to be enlightened.
For then I could learn the truth.

By admitting my failures and mistakes,
   I once more experience your mercy
   and know your compassion.
In truth, I am totally dependent on you

Quickly, gracious God,
grant me a clear knowledge of you.
Help me to grow in your grace.
Let me live in your life
   and speak your wisdom.

Rouse your steadfast and generous love.
Pour forth your abounding kindness.
You are always there to aid the fallen.
You are always there to lift up
   the people who cry out to you.
Show us your mercy and lift us up.
Infuse us with your Spirit of love.
You fill all creation with your care.
You will bring everything
   into union with you.
Yet you remain more than all creation.
You are always greater than the sum
   of all created things.

Teach me, O God.
The earth is full of your unshakable care.
Teach me compassion!
You have been so kind to me.
Form me in your mercy
   and give me good judgment,
   for I trust your wisdom.
Grant me knowledge of the right,
   for I know you are truth.

Unafraid, I will bless you, Holy One.
You assure me that you are with me.
You affirm your immense love for me.

You certify that I am connected
   with all things in you.
You show me that I am in you
   as you are in me.
You embody yourself in me.
As a surface wavelet is part of the ocean,
   you manifest yourself through me.
As a drop of vapor is a tiny part of a cloud,
   so I am a part of you.

Verily, I rejoice with all
   who reverence you.
I sing praise with those
   who truly worship you.
As they are, so let me be,
   and may my life inspire others
   to know and love you.

When I seek you, Holy One,
   help me to find you.
When I cry to you,
   once more answer my call.

Examine my heart, O God.
Your judgments are right.
Keep me faithful to your ways.
Let your abiding love be my only solace.
Let your mercy sustain me while I live.

You are my only delight!
Protect me from the snare of pride.
Do not let me be duped by deceit.
Help me to meditate on your precepts
   and keep me turned to you in every distress.

Zeal for your cause, O God, consumes me.
Let my heart be always open before you.
Let my tongue speak truthfully,
   so none are led astray.

120

How beaten down and angry I am.
How desperate and frustrated, I feel.
O God, I cry out to you. Answer me!

Save me from people who lie and cheat.
Rescue me from those who slander.
Deliver me from those who call good evil
    and say that evil is good.
Too long I have lived amid hostilities.
Too long I have dwelt
    surrounded by violence.
Gracious One, take pity on me.

Teach me, O God, and help me
    to confront deceit with clear truth,
    to return hatred with patient love,
    to oppose violence with calm serenity.
Let me be a bridge-builder across discord
    and a peacemaker among peoples.

Grant me an unshakable faith
    in your will for our good.
Give me an enduring trust
    in your work for our happiness
    amid a hostile and chaotic world.

121

Where can I look for help, O God?
Where shall I seek for solace?
My help is from you, Holy One.
You are my support and salvation.

You are always here to protect me.
You are continually alert to my need.
You are totally aware of my desires.
You do not slumber and never sleep.

You are my constant companion.
You are my devoted guardian.
You protect me from evil
    and uphold my life.

You know my coming in and going out.
You strengthen me in my labors
    and nourish me in my leisure.
Always and forever, you are near.

My God, I thank you.
I thank you every moment of every day.
I rejoice in you among your people.
I praise you for the people I know
    and for the people I will come to know.
I thank you for those I will never know,
    but you know in your abiding love.
You are enduring compassion.
Your faithful concern is never ending.

Let the glory of your greatness be seen.
Let the depth of your generosity be revealed.
By the saving power of your love, rescue us.
In the immensity of your wisdom, renew us.
Bring peace to our earth
    and tranquility to every human heart.

O God, speak your word of peace
    in the depths of our hearts.
Say to the tumult of this world: Peace!
Say amid the noise of our minds:
Be still! Know that I am your God!

Say in the depths of our souls:
　　Fear not! I love you!
Say to our fearful hearts:
　　You are my beloved little ones!
　　Come and partner me.
　　Come and be my companion.
　　Come and help me renew this earth.

Holy One, how deep our gratitude will be
　　when we really hear your words.
How great our joy will be
　　when we move to act on them.

Who, O God, will speak
　　of your magnanimous gifts?
Who will manifest your surging love
　　to our hurting world?

You have the final word.
You will never stop caring.
You will never stop forgiving.
You will never stop creating
　　and renewing the earth.

Nothing can deflect you
　　from accomplishing your purposes.
Nothing can defeat your plan.
Nothing will destroy the final fulfillment
　　of your desires.

Praise God, my soul!
My God, I will praise you!
Blessed be you, most gracious One.
Blessed be you, most generous One,
　　for you are the God who loves me.

122

I was glad when they said to me:
Let us go to the house of our God.
Let us enter God's temple with singing
    and come into God's presence with praise.

Our hearts are even now
    open to you, Most High.
O God, how great you are!
How wonderful your ways.
How beautiful your works.
How glorious your working out
    of our salvation.
How quickly you come to anyone
    who calls upon you.

To you, all the peoples
    of the earth will come.
They will come with grateful hearts
    and all will receive justice from you.
Your mercy extends to every generation.
Nothing good is ever lost from your hand.

O people, pray for the peace of our planet.
May all who love God prosper.
May those who work for good be blessed.
May peace flow as a mighty river
    and justice drop down like spring rain
    renewing the earth.

Yahweh, may your love be the sunlight
    illuminating our souls,
    and may your steadfast care
    be like honey inebriating our spirits
    with your exquisite sweetness.

May all creation be at peace with you.
For the sake of all who love you,
I ask your blessings for each of them.

123

Gracious God, to you we open our hearts.
To you we lift up our spirits.
Behold, as the eyes of servants
   are fixed on their employers,
   and the eyes of infants
   are fixed on their care givers,
   so our eyes are turned to you, great God,
   until you have mercy on us.

Have mercy on us, gracious One.
Have mercy on us, Holy One,
   for we are more than filled with sorrow.
We are more than surfeited
   with the mocking of unbelievers
   and the abuse of those who despise us.
Help us, most holy and living God.
We turn to you.

124

If Yahweh had not been with us.
Let God's people say:
   If Yahweh had not been with us,
   when our enemies attacked us,
   we would have been totally destroyed.

When their wrath blazed up against us,
  that fire storm would have
  burned us alive.
When the flood of their hatred
  surged over us,
  that torrent would have swept us away.
Blessed be our God who kept us safe.
We have escaped like a bird from a snare.
The snare is broken and we are free.
Our help is from the hand of Yahweh
  who made the heavens and the earth.

125

Those who trust in Yahweh
  are like mountains.
They are like mountains
  which cannot be moved and abide forever.
As the atmosphere surrounds this globe
  and sustains all life on our planet,
  so Yahweh enfolds the peoples of earth.
Yahweh brings good from every situation.
  and sustains our lives for now and always.

Therefore evil shall never be victorious.
Pain and sorrow shall pass away.
Comfort shall come to the afflicted
  and consolation shall fill the oppressed.

O God, be kind to those who do good.
Grant your favor to the upright of heart.
Convert those who follow crooked ways
  and turn them from self destruction.
Let your your peace be upon our world
  and may your love dwell in our hearts.

126

When Yahweh restored us to life
  we were like people dreaming.
When we were freed from sin
  and redeemed from guilt
  we were overwhelmed with joy.

Then our mouths were filled with laughter
  and our tongues with rejoicing.
Then the nations said to each other:
Yahweh has done great things for them.
Yahweh has done great things for us.
We were glad, indeed.

O Holy One, continue to restore our lives.
As a desert wadi can quickly fill with water,
  change our fortunes to fullness of delight

May those who sow in tears
  reap with shouts of delight.
May they who go forth weeping,
  bearing their good works to be sown,
  come home rejoicing,
  carrying their blessings with gladness.
Then all will see and give thanks.

127

Unless Yahweh builds the house,
  they labor in vain who build it.
Unless Yahweh protects the city,
  the guard keeps watch in vain.

It is futile to rise early and sit up late,
  you who eat hard-earned bread.
For even in the hours of sleep
Yahweh generously provides for us.

See and count your blessings.
Do you have breath and bed and bread?
Do your eyes see and ears hear?
Do your legs move and your mind work?
Are your loved ones near to you?

Happy are the people
  who remember their blessings.
Happy are the ones
  who give thanks for them.
They shall walk with integrity
  in the land of the living.
Their place is established forever.

128

Fortunate the people
  who reverence Yahweh.
You who walk in God's ways are secure.
You shall eat of the fruit of your labors.
You shall be content
  and matters shall go well for you.
Your spouse will be a source of joy.
Your family will be a fruitful vine
  providing merriment and delight.
Your children will be like fruit trees
  giving you many satisfactions.
Thus they who reverence Yahweh
  shall be blessed.

May God bless your days
  with prosperity
  and your heart with peace.
May you be blessed
  all the days of your life.

May you live to see the achievement
  of your dearest desires.
May the fulfillment
  of a good marriage be yours
  and may you live to enjoy
  the laughter of your grandchildren.
May God's peace be upon all of us.

129

Often I have been afflicted.
I have known troubles from my youth.
Yes, let me now say:
I have often seen sorrow.
I have often been filled with pain.
But I was not overcome.

Sorrow, hunger, and beatings
  have been my lot.
Hostility and betrayal
  have followed after me.
But God has freed me from these woes.
Yahweh has cut the cords of my afflictions.

Help me to love, O God,
  even when I am not loved.
Help me to respond with tranquility,
  even to those who seek to injure me.

Grant justice to the oppressed
   and conversion of heart
   to their oppressors.

Let all who pass by say:
   May the blessing of Yahweh be upon you.
We bless you in the name of our God.

130

O God, again I have failed.
Once more I have sinned and cry out to you.
Holy One, if you remembered failures,
   who could stand before you?
If you remembered sins,
   who would escape condemnation?

Yahweh, I know you are mercy.
I know you are abounding kindness.
So I cry out to you for forgiveness
   and wait for your help.
I trust in your steadfast mercy.
I hope in You-Who-Are.

More than a watchman looks
   for the light of dawn,
I eagerly wait for you.
More than the starving
   think obsessively of food,
I yearn for your mercy
   and wait for your help.

O peoples of the earth,
   hope in Yahweh!
   For the Holy One is enduring love.

Yahweh is always willing to save.
Yahweh is always willing to forgive
   a repentant heart.
This great and gracious One
   will rescue us from our failures
   and redeem us from all our sins.

Blessed be our God!

131

Gracious One, my heart is not proud
   nor are my desires set on great things.
I do not involve myself
   either in important affairs
   or in things too complicated for me.

Truly I have calmed my mind.
I have quieted my soul.
As a little child on its mother's lap
   so is my soul within me.

O you peoples of the earth,
   hope in the holy One-Who-Is.
Hope in this gracious Mystery,
   both now and forever.

132

Holy One, we remember your saints.
We remember the people
   who followed your way.

We remember the hardships
   they chose to endure
   and your promise to be with them always.

O Beloved One, we still need
   your presence with us.
We need your love
   and your grace to inspire us.
We need your support
   so we may conform our lives
   to your desires for us.
Help us to trust you
   and to come to you.

Keep us faithful to your ways.
Help us to follow your lead.
Keep us as unwavering in our love for you
   as you are unwavering in your love for us.
Help us to follow your example
   through the love and service
   we give to one another.

Come! Let us go to Yahweh.
Let us worship our God
   with joy and thanksgiving.
Let us enter God's presence with song
   for Yahweh is good and merciful to all.

Great God, you made a promise to David.
You promised his descendent would come.
An offspring would come to save humanity
   and bring your people back to you.
You kept your promise, Holy One.
Jesus is the promised offspring.
He is David's heir and our savior.

O God, Jesus was faithful to you.
Jesus freely shows your love for us.

Jesus gives us his very life with you.
He is the fullness of Who-You-Are.
Blessed be this gift and this giver.
Blessed be Yahweh,
    the One-Who-Is, forever.

Yahweh, you chose this tiny planet.
You are Holy presence in all of creation.
You remain the deepest part of all things
    yet are always beyond all things.
Thus says Yahweh, our God:
This is where I will always be.
Nothing will separate me
    from my creations.
I perpetually bless this world and its peoples.

I am especially mindful of the poor.
I am particularly present to the despised.
I provide for all needs in due season.
I will lift up leaders who do what is right.
I will bless all they do.
I will raise up priests to lead my people
    in my spirit and my truth.

My people will sing for joy.
They will shout with gladness
    because I preserve the just
    and guard the upright of heart.

I keep watch over them
    for all of their lives
    and preserve them with me forever.

133

How marvelous it is and how joyful
  when humanity lives in peace
How beautiful and how satisfying
  when people are united in love.

How glorious it is when kindliness blooms
  like spring flowers after winter snows,
  and how delightful when charity flows
  as a tranquil river under a summer sun.

This is a precious comfort
  that warms the heart.
It is satisfaction to the spirit,
  more filling than the finest food.

It is a soothing balm to the soul,
  sweeter than sugar
  or honey from the comb.
It is an overwhelming joy,
  like a sparkling wine
  that inebriates the soul.

Such concord is a gift from Yahweh.
It is a gift and a blessing beyond all price.
Gracious One, you give this great gift
  to those who accept it.
You give it freely forever. Alleluia.

134

Come! Bless our God,
   all you peoples of Yahweh
   who live in the Holy One's presence,
   and stand in this gracious One's love.

Lift up your hands in praise.
Lift up your hearts in gratitude.
Bless our God, the One-Who-Is.

May Yahweh, the creator
   and sustainer of all that is,
   bless you and keep you secure,
   always and forevermore.

135

Praise to our God!
Exult, you little ones of Yahweh.
Give praise to this gracious Mystery.

Give adoration and thanksgiving,
   you who live in God's love.
Give reverence and honor,
   you who live in God's presence

Praise Yahweh, for God is good.
Sing your gladness to the gracious One,
   for our God is generous and merciful.

Holy One, you continually choose us.
It is not we who choose you.
You made us to be your own.

You always do what is good
   and work for the total fulfillment
   of all things in creation,
   yesterday, today, and forever.

I know Yahweh is great.
Our God is above every image.
Yahweh is greater than all thoughts.

Gracious One, you do what pleases you.
You establish the deeps of space
   and hold this little planet
   in the palm of your hand.

You create the seas
   and bring forth the clouds.
You release lightning
   and send rain.
You dispatch the winds
   and calm the storms.
You are the source
   and sustainer of all life.

Again and again
   you pour out signs for us.
You perform wonders for us.
You free us from every kind of slavery.
You release us from every kind of sin.

You give us a heritage in you.
You give us life in your Life,
   through the life and death and rising
   of your Beloved One, Jesus the Christ.

Your goodness, great God, endures forever.
Your steadfast love is seen in every age.
You vindicate your little ones
   and have compassion on all flesh.

The idols of this world
   are money and power and fame.
They are the work of human desire.
They grow from human frailty.
Their source is human fear.

But these idols provide neither safety
   nor freedom from fear.
They disappear like morning fog
   which melts away in the rising sun.

O people of Yahweh, bless our God.
O little ones of Yahweh, bless our God.
O servants of Yahweh, bless our God.
O you who reverence Yahweh,
   bless our God.
Blessed be our God
   by every heart and mind and spirit
   through all generations.
May we praise our God forever.

136

We thank you, Yahweh, for you are good.
For your love endures forever.
You alone do great deeds;
   You alone do wondrous works.
For your love endures forever.

You made the heavens
   and formed the earth.
For your love endures forever.
You spread out the seas
   and clothed the dry land.
For your love endures forever.

You made the sun to mark the day.
For your love endures forever.
You set the moon and stars
   to govern the night.
For your love endures forever.

You brought forth self-aware beings
   from the dust of the earth.
For your love endures forever.
You shepherded humankind
   with faithful care.
For your love endures forever.

Through thousands of years
   you were with them.
You kept them close to you
   through the ravages of earthquakes,
   fires, and floods.
For your love endures forever.
You always saved a remnant for yourself
   through every war and famine and plague.
For your love endures forever.

You inspired the peoples
   to explore and learn.
For your love endures forever.
You encouraged them
   to improve hunting skills
   and discover healing methods.
For your love endures forever.

You motivated tribes and nations
   to develop agriculture
   and advance farming processes.
For your love endures forever.
You stimulated these to create new words
   and imagine new ideas.
For your love endures forever.

You sparked the discovery of weaving,
and the development of pottery.
For your love endures forever.
You encouraged the evolution
of mathematics, art, and music.
For your love endures forever.

You supported the creation of writing
and the quest for new building techniques.
For your love endures forever.
You stirred the desire for learning
and the ability to imagine.
For your love endures forever.

You were always seeking
to improve the peoples' lives.
For your love endures forever.
So you sent teachers to teach them
and prophets to lead them.
For your love endures forever.
And in time you called forth
a tiny tribe of people
For your love endures forever.

You led them and formed them
through many generations.
For your love endures forever.
You helped them to grow
in knowledge and awareness of you.
For your love endures forever.

Then, in the fullness of time,
you brought forth a child
from these people.
For your love endures forever.
This child, born of a woman,
was your visible presence-with-us.
For your love endures forever.

And this child, grown to adulthood,
   is your wisdom and your grace with us.
For your love endures forever.
This child shows us
Who-You-Are
   and who we are
   in ways that we can understand.
For your love endures forever.

Holy One, this child calls us
   from death to new life in you.
For your love endures forever.
This child calls each of us
   to live your compassion
   and to serve one another.
For your love endures forever.

This child calls each human being
   to partner you in your enterprise of love.
For your love endures forever.
We thank you, Yahweh,
   for such an immense gift,
   for such a wonderful blessing.
Your love, indeed, endures forever.

137

Great God, we grieved our loss
   when we remembered you.
Afflictions were our heritage.
Sadness was our food and drink
   when we recalled our past.
O God, we remembered
   turning away from you.

We remembered losing our awareness
   of your presence with us.
So we sat down and wept.
Immense sorrow overcame us.
Nothing could assuage our woe.
We turned away from comfort
   and refused all solace.

When some asked us for laughter
   and others asked for dancing,
   we could not do it.
O God, we would not ignore our loss.
Gracious One, we could not forget you.

Yahweh, may we never depart from you.
May we always remember you.
May we place you above
   our greatest delights.
May we put you before
   all else we hold dear.
O merciful One, remember us
   in the midst of our pain and sorrow.

138

O God, how I yearn for you to finish
   the work you started.
How I desire for you to complete
   the task you labored to accomplish.
It is a plan you envisioned
   from before the beginning.

My heart is bursting with joy
   and my mouth is filled with rejoicing
   when I ponder your creation.

When I think of your saving acts,
  I give you thanks with all my being.

I will sing your praise
  before all peoples.
I reverence and adore you
  in the temple of my spirit.
I bow down before you
  and give you thanks
  for your great mercy on all flesh.
I rejoice in your faithfulness.
Your will and word are supreme.

On the day I called out to you,
  you answered me.
You gave me strength and courage.
You lifted me from distress.
When I was floundering
  in the midst of troubles,
  you saved me and preserved me.
You delivered me from fear.

All the great of the earth will praise you.
All your little ones will bless you.
They heard and believed
  your mighty promises.
Each will sing of your marvelous works.
They will tell of your great glory.
For you are always close to the lowly.
But you abandon the proud
  to their vanities.

You will accomplish your purposes.
You will fulfill your desires.
You are faithful to your promises
  and your love abides forever.
Great God, complete the work
  that you have begun!

139

Holy and beloved One,
   you formed me and you know me.
You know when I sit and when I stand.
You know my coming in and my going out.

You know my thoughts
   even before I think them.
You know my every word
   even before I speak them.
You know all my desires
   even before I know them.

You are utterly aware of all that I am.
You encompass my whole being
   in your loving embrace.
Such knowledge is too deep for me.
It totally exceeds my ability to comprehend.

Where can I go to escape you?
Where can I flee from your presence?
If I fly to the highest mountains,
   you are there.
If I dive to the depths of the oceans,
   you are still there.
If I flee to the ends of the earth,
   even there you are present
   to teach and guide me.

Should I ask the darkness to hide me
   or the light of day to become pitch black,
   it would not matter to you, O God.
For, gracious One, the darkness
   is not dark to you,
   and the blackness of a black hole
   is lighter than day.

Holy One, you formed my inmost being.
You were present at my creation.
You formed the unique genetic code
   that creates my body.
You were intimately involved
   as I grew in my mother's womb.
You beheld me before I was born.
You knew me before I was formed.

Marvelous are your works, O God.
It is clear to me that even my bones
   are not hidden from you.
You saw all my days
   before one of them had come to be.

You are actively present
   in every moment of my life.
I am amazed and praise you
   for such a great and generous gift.

How deep are your works, great God.
How vast the sum of your creations.
I try to count them
   and they are more than the sands of the sea.
For even if I might count these grains,
I would still not come to the end
   of the number of your works.

O gracious and beloved One, how I wish
   human grief and pain would disappear.
How I desire that kindness would multiply
   and malice cease to be.
How I weep to see the injuries
   that we inflict on one another.
How I hurt to see people mock you.
And how I grieve
   when I see your little ones reviled.

O God, turn us to your ways!
Transform us so we may eagerly follow
   your paths of joy-filled life.
Let every person see
   you are the way to everlasting bliss.
Let the peoples praise you!
Let all the peoples praise you!

140

Beloved One, preserve us
   from the willful evil that some do,
   and shelter us from the evil
   that others do unaware.

Protect us from those who plan violence.
Guard us from those who stir up malice.
Defend us from those who provoke enmity
   and make anger their constant companion.
Shield us from those who embrace hatred
   as a familiar friend.

The tongue becomes a sharp dagger
   when people are filled with anger
   and lips spread deadly poison
   when people are filled with envy.

Preserve us, O God, from wickedness
   and deliver us from violence.
Keep us from becoming trapped
   in webs of malice and wrath.
Screen us from the arrows of spite
   and save us from the injuries of deceit.

Gracious One, you are our God.
You are the One whom we reverence.
You are the great and gracious Mystery
   whom we respect and love.

Holy One, you are the center of my spirit
   and the whole desire of my soul.
Hear my cry!
You are my strong deliverer.
You have kept me safe
   and cut the bonds of evil that held me.
Let wickedness vanish
   and sin be no more.
May violence disappear
   and deceit be exposed.
Keep malice from finding a home
   in the human heart.

Beloved One, I know you uphold
   the cause of the needy.
I know you seek justice for the poor.
Surely those who love you will praise you.
They who follow your paths
   will live in your presence, forever.

141

When I call, great God, hear me!
Help me, gracious One.
Let my prayer rise
   like incense before you.
See my lifted hands
   as an offering of praise.

Holy One, place a guard on my mouth.
Keep a sentry at the door of my lips.
Do not let me speak foolishly or angrily.
Keep my heart from foolish desires
   and my mind from wicked thoughts.
Do not permit me to keep company
   with vicious ideas
   nor allow me to dine with sinful attitudes.

Let righteousness correct me
   and faithfulness restore me.
May the gift of your grace
   save me from evil deeds
   and the grace of your presence
   always be with me.
May evil in all its forms
   be thrown down
   and all the peoples turn to you
   in heartfelt gratitude,
   because of your mercy
   and faithful love.

Gracious and glorious One,
   my eyes are turned to you, .
My heart reaches out to you.
My spirit seeks refuge in you.
You are my hope and my joy
   and I am secure in you.
You will protect me
   from the traps of anger and envy
   by which we are so easily snared.
You will save me
   from the pitfalls of greed and pride,
   into which we so easily plunge.

Thank you, most loving One,
   for your great mercy.
   I shall not be harmed.

142

O God, I am so very weary
 and I feel terribly depressed.
I am troubled and lonely.
Again I turn to you for help.
I call out to you in prayer.
I pour out my problems before you
 and I tell you all my troubles.
When I am assaulted by fear
 and vacillate in doubt,
 you know what I should do.
Show me the way to go.

My path is full of traps and snares.
I could easily stumble and fall.
There is no one to help me
 except you.
No one takes notice
 and no one cares.

Great God, I cry out to you.
Help me! For you are my protection.
My God, you are my life.
You are my all.
Listen to my call
 for I am brought very low.

Save me, O God, from this darkness.
Pull me from this despair.
It is too strong for me.
Bring me out of this fearful prison.
Then I will give you thanks
 with all your people.
I will praise you with them
 because of your goodness to me.

143

Great and gracious One,
   listen to my prayer.
In your great goodness,
   hear my plea.
Because you are faithful,
   answer me.
O God, do not judge me,
   for before you no one can stand.

Holy One, my failures haunt me.
My sins overwhelm me.
I sit as one lost in a dark cave.
I am like a ghost.
There is no place for me
   in the land of the living.
I feel ready to die.
I am flooded with despair.
O God, do not judge me,
   for before you no one can stand.

I remember days gone by.
I think of your wonderful works.
I meditate on all your deeds.
I stretch out my hands to you.
My spirit longs for you
   as one adrift at sea longs for land.
O God, do not judge me,
   for before you no one can stand.

Answer me, O God!
   For my spirit fails.
Do not hide yourself from me
   for I am as one drowning.

Once more let me feel your solace.
Let me know your companionship
   for I put my trust in you.
Teach me the way to go.
I commit my whole being to your care.
O God, do not judge me,
   for before you no one can stand.

I turn to you for strength and for courage.
I turn to you for wisdom and for truth.
Rescue me as you have promised.
In your goodness, save me from despair.
Because of your love for me
   grant me new life.

O God, do not judge me,
   for before you no one can stand.
O God, to you I turn.
My God, for you I wait.

144

Blessed be you, most Holy One.
You are my safe haven.
You train my mind to understand
   and my spirit to comprehend.
You are my only security.
You are my refuge and my deliverer.
You protect me in times of danger.
You preserve me in times of distress.

Gracious One, what are we
   that you think of us?
Who are human beings
   that you care for us?

We are but a single breath.
Our lives are quickly spent.
Our days are but a passing shadow,
    here and gone.

Come, Holy One! Come into our souls.
Touch our hearts with the fire of your love.
Touch our spirits with your mercy
    and compassionate care.

You who created the lightning flash
    can rescue me from tribulation.
You who raised up the mountains
    and set the limits of the seas
    can save me from every evil.

Holy One, rescue me from all that binds me
    and deliver me from all that is false.
Then, O God, I will sing you a new song.
I will raise my hands in thanksgiving.
I will play melodies of joyful gratitude
    for you have set me free.

You released me from the snare of anger
    and saved me from the trap of indolence.
You shielded me from the pitfall of envy
    and liberated from the meshes of greed.

You kept me from the entanglements of lust
    and freed me from the hook of gluttony.
You defended me from the perfidy of pride
    and protected me from the daggers of doubt.
You lifted me from the anguish of despair.

May all of us be blessed by your peace.
May we know the joy of happy families.
May our hearts be filled with generosity
    and our minds with loving thoughts.

May the work of our hands
   heal and prosper our world.
May there be no fear or want
   and may there be no cry of distress
   in all the land.

Happy the people upon whom
   these blessings fall.
Happy the people whose God is Yahweh.

145

Great is Yahweh!
How wonderful is our God.

Most high and glorious One,
   we proclaim your greatness.
Everyday we thank you.
We will praise you forever and ever.

Yahweh, you are so marvelous.
Your thoughts are vastly deeper
   than our thoughts.
Your works are immensely greater
   than our ability to understand.

Most high and glorious One,
   how great you are!
You will be reverenced
   forever and ever.
Your works will be declared
   from generation to generation.

Most high and glorious One,
   how great you are!

Your wondrous deeds will be proclaimed
    in the assemblies of the peoples.

I will constantly meditate
    on your mercy.
I will declare your goodness to all
    who will listen.
I will constantly sing of your kindness
    poured out on all creatures.

O God, you are gracious and merciful.
You are abounding in steadfast love.
You are good to all peoples.
You have compassion upon everyone
    and careful concern for everything.

Great are you, most high and glorious One.
All creatures shall praise you.
Your faithful little ones shall bless you.
They will tell of your amazing kindness.
They will proclaim the glories of your gifts.
They will manifest the radiant wonder
    of your presence with us.

Your presence continues
    in all generations.
You establish our at-one-ment with you
    and with each other.
You are faithful in all your words
    and gracious in all your works.
You answer all who call upon you
    and lift up anyone who has fallen.

Great God, our eyes look to you with hope.
You provide for us in due season.
We receive enough, and more than enough.
You satisfy the needs of every living thing.
O God, you are just in all your ways.

You are merciful in all your actions.
You are ever near to your creation.
You make your presence known
   to all who call upon you.

You open your hands to everyone
   who reverences you.
You provide for the needs
   of the people who honor you.
You rescue anyone who calls upon you
   with a sincere and humble heart.
You watch over all peoples with immense love.

You take care of each creature
   and safeguard your little ones.
Amazingly, you are ever working
   to turn even the ones who do evil
   away from sin.
You are forever striving
   to keep even the wicked
   from destroying themselves.

Yahweh, we shall always praise you.
All creatures will praise and bless you
   forever and ever.

146

O God, I adore you!
I rejoice in your goodness
   and praise you for your love.
I shall thank you with great gladness
   for as long as I live.
I will sing your praises every day of my life.

When we die, O God, we return to the dust.
On that day all our hopes and dreams,
    our plans and property, pass on to others.
Therefore do not put your trust
    in people or in things.
People are mortal and plans go awry,
    while things are so easily destroyed.
Rather, trust in Yahweh who is eternal.

O God, you keep faith forever.
You bring forth justice for the oppressed.
You provide food for the hungry.
You set prisoners free
    and give sight to the blind.

You lift up those who have fallen
    and embrace the righteous with tender care.
You protect strangers and help the helpless.
But selfishness and evil actions lead to ruin.

Our God is God for all generations.
I praise and rejoice in you, O God!

147

Praise Yahweh, O nations.
Praise the One-Who-Is, O peoples.
For Yahweh gives you vision
    and is your hope of joy.

The Holy One pours out mercy
    and blesses your children.
Yahweh establishes peace in the land
    and fills you with the finest food.

Our God works in every circumstance.
At Yahweh's bidding
    the winds blow and the waters flow.
Spring and summer, fall and winter,
    the rhythms of daily life
    and the seasons of our lives
    show forth God's provident goodness.

Yahweh's wisdom/word is sent out.
Swiftly it runs, seeking open hearts
    and willing souls
God's goodness is seen in open hearts.
The Holy Mystery's greatness is shown
    through willing souls.
Yahweh faithfully shepherds these people
    and gently holds them very close.

Only those who seek Yahweh
    and follow after God's wisdom/word
    with open hearts and willing souls
    will find the One they seek in pure joy.

148

Praise Yahweh from the heavens.
Extol Yahweh in the heights.
Glorify the One-Who-Is, all you angels.
Worship the gracious One, all you hosts.
Adore the Holy One, you highest heavens.
Acclaim the merciful One,
    you deepest depths.

Let all that is, praise our God.
For Yahweh commanded
    and they were created.

God established them forever and ever.
Yahweh made a covenant with creation
   which shall not be revoked.

Praise Yahweh all the earth.
Reverence the gracious One,
   all you elements.
Fire and hail, snow and fog,
stormy winds and gentle breezes,
mountains and all hills,
fruit trees and all evergreens.
Let everything honor our God forever.

Worship the glorious One,
   all you creatures of the earth:
   wild beasts and tame animals,
   all reptiles and winged creatures,
   leaders of the earth and all peoples,
   all thinkers and judges of the earth,
   young men and maidens,
   old men and women and children, too.
Let all adore our God.
For Yahweh alone is sublime.

Holy One, your glory
   is above our understanding.
The wonder of you is beyond
   our greatest imaginings.

You have blessed your people.
Let praise fill the hearts
   of your faithful ones.
Bless the children
   and hold your people
   very close to your heart.

149

We praise you, O God,
  and we thank you.
We will sing a new song
  in the assembly of your people.
We rejoice in you who are our creator.
We are glad in you
  who are our liberator.
Let all your peoples rejoice!
Let all creation sing with gladness!

We declare your goodness with dancing.
We proclaim your greatness with song
    for you find joy in the joy of your people
    and take great pleasure in your creation.
You adorn the humble with honor
    while you turn away the proud.

O God, we give thanks for your generosity.
Let your faithful little ones exalt in glory.
Let them sing throughout the night.
May each be filled with delight
    and, as the new day dawns,
    may high praise be in their throats
    to you, most gracious One.

Keep us ardently steadfast in your paths.
May we faithfully follow your ways
    of wisdom and compassion.
Let hatred and greed be no more.
Let violence melt away
    like the morning mist.
Let pride vanish like smoke
    and greed disappear like
    water among desert sands.

This is the glory of your faithful little ones.
They are like you, gracious One,
    steadfast and generous and true.
Great God, we praise you!

150

Praise Yahweh, all you peoples!
Praise Yahweh, all you nations!
Praise Yahweh, all the earth!
We praise you in the sanctuary of our hearts.
We praise you for your marvelous creation.
We praise you for your saving deeds.

We praise you
    for your surpassing greatness.
We praise you
    for you infinite wisdom.
We praise you
    for your deep, mysterious love.

Praise Yahweh
    with melody and with singing.
Praise Yahweh
    with laughter and with dancing.

We praise you with the harp
    and trumpet.
We praise you with pipes
    and tambourines.
We praise you with drums and cymbals.
We praise you with all our hearts.

Praise Yahweh, all you peoples!
Let everything that breathes praise our God.